Mary

How to Live Above Your Circumstances and Beyond Yourself

over
it

Over iT

How to Live Above Your
Circumstances and Beyond Yourself

Published by SPARK Publications
Cover design, page design and production by SPARK Publications
SPARKPublications.com

ISBN: 978-0-9854070-1-8

Contact the author at:
Mary@MaryBuchan.com or MaryBuchan.com

Printed in the United States of America.

Dedication

Dedicated to women everywhere who are committed to overcoming any circumstances that keep them from being their authentic selves. You are overcomers. You are mothers and wives and sisters. You are business women and homemakers and dreamers. You are visionaries and volunteers. You are artists and musicians and poets and advocates for creating the best possible world.

My wish for you is to use this book to help you in your journey to peace, health, and wholeness, leading you to an amazing new oasis of fulfillment and fruitfulness.

This book was written with special appreciation for my amazing kids, Molly, Abbie, and Ben. You've grown from delightful children into beautiful adults. You are beaming lights in God's universe, and I am so very proud of you.

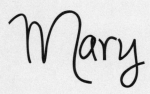

Endorsements

"…a great book of wisdom, wit, and tremendous hope…"
— **Stephen Arterburn**, radio talk-show host,
best-selling author, and founder of
New Life Ministries and Women of Faith

*"Mary Buchan…equips you with perspective and insight…
a must-read…"*

— **Kathrine Lee**, founder of
The Ultimate Source

"Read and be uplifted!"

— **Leighton Ford**, founder and president
of Leighton Ford Ministries

Contents

It's so good to
be free from the
heaviness

Unlocking Our Spirits

"One is not born a woman, one becomes one."
– Simone de Beauvoir

Throughout my life, my dad has always insisted, "Don't judge someone until you walk a mile in their shoes."

Women tend to do this instinctively. We share our journeys. We carry each other's emotional baggage and get over it by healing together. We live above our circumstances by becoming leaders and guides and encouragers for each other. We grow beyond ourselves and fall in love and give birth and express our gifts in an exciting yet sometimes unraveling world that continues to challenge us.

We're up to the challenge!

I spent my early years as a shy introvert, growing into a late bloomer who constantly wrestled with a lack of confidence. Imagine a turtle peeping timidly out of its shell, making sure it's safe, then taking a few hesitant steps until faced with the next challenge—that was me.

But there's another side to my shy nature. I'm also a daredevil.

Even as a child, I liked to take risks, do pranks, and get into trouble with my friends. And as my cousin Judy reminded me recently, I often was the ringleader of our shenanigans. A bit hyperactive, I was always on the go. I enjoyed hopping, skipping, jumping, running, tumbling, climbing, swimming, and riding my bike. And I loved to sing.

A lot of us are like that—we're a complicated mix of contradictory traits. Many of us have a little bit of the rebel in us, or traits that make us wonder how we really fit into this world. That makes me want to stand up and cheer every time I read the text of this famous Steve Jobs ad for Apple products:

Here's to the crazy ones, the misfits, the rebels, the troublemakers, the round pegs in the square holes... the ones who see things differently—they're not fond of rules... You can quote them, disagree with them, glorify or vilify them, but the only thing you can't do is ignore them because they change things...they push the human race forward, and while some may see them as the crazy ones, we see genius, because the ones who are crazy enough to think that they can change the world, are the ones who do.

I plead guilty. Yes, I'm a "crazy one," a misfit, a troublemaker, and a round peg in a square hole. I definitely see things differently and am not fond of rules. How about you? One way or the other, women have never been better equipped to "push the human race forward." We can change the world!

But not without some pain.

I love the old nursery rhyme "Mary, Mary, Quite Contrary," which raises the question of how her garden will grow. Well, in the case of *this* Mary, my growth has come through Miracle Grow. You see, breaking free from my past has truly been nothing short of a miracle, though it has taken a great deal of work and prayer. I've faced times when I felt hopeless—trapped and in a rut with no way out. As many of us have, I've felt paralyzed by fear and insecurity. I've let the past define me and the future intimidate me.

Sometimes that timid-turtle part of me, peeping out of its shell, seemed in danger of controlling my life; sometimes the rebel seemed to have me headed completely out of control.

In spite of a difficult past and my present shortcomings, I'm blessed to be leading a life of joy and abundance today. I'm grateful for every opportunity to soar—to get over it—that is sent my way to make me the person I am today.

Over the years, sometimes in spite of myself, I've managed to unlock my spirit and transform myself.

But I didn't do it alone.

As I share stories from my life and the lessons I've learned along the way, I encourage you to consider the stories that have changed your life. What experiences and life-lessons have made you the person you are today? What enables you to live above your circumstances and beyond yourself in this unraveling world? Equally important, what beliefs and experiences still keep your spirit under lock and key? The things that hold you back from being the best that you can be?

For me, this journey to be the best I can be has been a divine quest all the way. The right people, books, angels, and opportunities have always manifested at just the right times. I needed help navigating rough waters on my way to wholeness and happiness—help that so often came to me through my community of other women.

What about you?

Just reading about my journey won't make *your* journey an enlightening or transformative experience. Why not start a personal journal about your journey, as a way to talk to yourself—your authentic self? You'll find questions at the end of each chapter to guide your journaling, but feel free to follow your own inner prompts as you journal.

- As you think back on your journey in life so far, what are two of your most pivotal experiences—maybe one from childhood and one from early adulthood? Who was involved? How did you feel? What lessons did you take away from those experiences?

- Do you see those experiences differently today? How might you view those experiences if you imagine they happened instead to a child you know? What would you say if a young girl came to you today for wisdom or advice about similar situations?

- Do you feel good enough about the road you've traveled that you would be willing to invite others to "walk in your shoes"? Why or why not?

The weight's
been lifted off

Side Trips and Dead-Ends on the Road to Well-Being

"People are like stained-glass windows. They sparkle and shine when the sun is out, but when the darkness sets in, their true beauty is revealed only if there is a light from within."
- Elizabeth Kubler-Ross

Each decade of life seems to carry its own epiphany. During that decade between 10 and 20, for example, I discovered that boys really did make a positive contribution to the universe. Between 20 and 30, I learned that, just like my parents always said, money does not grow on trees. From 30 to 40, I learned the joys—and the agonies—of parenting.

The biggest changes of all started when I was 40. That's when I learned that my mother had not ruined my life and my husband could not fix my life.

Before that, I was pretty angry at times for all the nurturing and unconditional love I believed I had not received from my mom. Up until that point, I blamed mom for just about all the ways my life was imperfect.

I see it differently today, of course. It is always difficult to share family secrets and I have struggled with whether or not to share mine in this book. Quite frankly, I am tired of pretending that my personal struggle as a child had no effect on me. Decades later and years of counseling have proven that I had to learn how to get Over many "Its" so that I could live above my circumstances and beyond myself.

You see, Mom suffered from bi-polar disorder and several other mental illnesses. In those days, when it was diagnosed at all, it was called manic depression. Also in those days, there was virtually no effective treatment for a mental disorder that made life a living hell for the people who suffered from it and for the people who loved them and tried to live with them.

Sometimes Mom was too depressed to get out of bed, much less do the hundreds of things mothers are expected to do to keep a household running. Other times, her manic states drove her to rage or other irrational behavior that children have no way of understanding or protecting themselves from.

In other words, my childhood wasn't perfect.

For a long time, I thought yours must have been perfect. I spent a lot of years angry about how unfair that was. Since then, I've learned that very few of us grew up in an episode of "Father Knows Best" or "The Brady Bunch."

I was in my 40s before I realized that my mother did the best she could. I forgave her and my father for my imperfect childhood. Finally, I even realized that I could be forgiven for blaming them for circumstances they certainly would have changed if they could have.

Becoming a mother myself and realizing how hard it is to get it right was a big part of my healing journey. I started to recognize that I was doing the best I could and that, even without the degree of health issues my mother had faced, I was far from a perfect mother. In fact, at times I was pretty much a wreck because I still hadn't managed to get over my own far-from-perfect childhood.

Because of the circumstances I grew up in, I spent many years doubting whether true well-being was even possible in this life. And even if well-being was a possibility for others, I was skeptical that it would be given to me. Maybe, I reasoned, I was just destined to have a messy, unraveling, and sometimes painful life.

I've also spent much of my life looking for well-being in the wrong places. I thought that if I had the right husband, right house, right job, right church, right friends, and right investments, I would feel satisfied inside. Then all the external trappings of my life fell apart and I realized that all of those things were really only side trips and dead ends on the road to well-being.

Life has taught me that true contentment is an inside job.

Ironically, a true sense of well-being began not when my circumstances were at their best, but when it seemed that the bottom was falling out of my life. My husband was between jobs. We had to move out of a house I really loved. I needed to go back to work as a nurse. Our financial future looked very cloudy.

And yet, even during those uncertain times, I experienced amazing peace as a gift from God — because I had quit expecting my happiness to come from people and things.

In his book *Flourish*, Martin Seligman identifies five key components of a vibrant life: positive emotion, engagement, relationships, meaning, and accomplishment. All of these are vital ingredients to help us flourish as individuals—and all of them are spiritual attributes available to every one of us.

Sometimes I still pinch myself to make sure I'm not dreaming and won't wake up again to the sadness and turmoil I experienced before. But no, my well-being is real, and it is a gift from God, who taught me how to live above my circumstances and beyond myself. Since the world didn't give it to me, the world can't take it away.

What about you?

- What people or circumstances have you blamed for your less-than-perfect life?

- Journal about some of the dead ends and side trips you've traveled in your search for well-being.

- How would you rate your life today on Martin Seligman's five key components of a vibrant life: positive emotion, engagement, relationships, meaning, and accomplishment. What other components might you add to that list?

He's filled the
emptiness

Duck Feathers

*"Reality is the leading cause of stress
among those in touch with it."*
– Lily Tomlin

D ucks never feel wet.

Although they spend most of their time in lakes, ponds and rivers, ducks never seem to need someone to throw them a towel. Why? Ducks have been given an oily coating on their feathers to keep those feathers from absorbing all that water.

Wouldn't it be nice if we had some duck feathers to protect us from the storms of life?

I grew up as a sensitive sort, often taking life and myself much too seriously. When my friend Amy teased me, I never laughed. Sometimes I wanted to cry. Sometimes I wanted to march off in a huff or hide my face in embarrassment. In frustration, Amy would ask me, "Mary, can't you take a joke?!"

No, I definitely couldn't.

When faced with annoying events or critical comments from people around me, I often worked myself into a tizzy. Needless to say, my overreactions caused plenty of friction between others and me, especially with the people I love. I finally started to wonder how I could turn down my sensitivity meter.

By the time I was a newlywed and a recent graduate from nursing school, it was painfully clear that my hypersensitivity was hindering me from enjoying life. Instead of rolling with the punches life threw my way, I took everything personally. Even minor incidents could rock my emotional equilibrium for days.

Then one day, my husband told me how ducks manage to keep their feathers dry and unruffled. Because of the special oil on their feathers, the water simply beads up and slides off.

He told me that's how I needed to view the stressors in my life. Instead of allowing them to soak into my spirit and rock my emotions, I needed to picture them simply rolling off my back.

So when I caught myself taking anything too seriously, I began to mentally cloak myself in duck feathers. When faced with an angry boss, anxious coworker, rude patient, irritable friend, or just my own fears, I pictured water flowing off my feathers as I floated in a peaceful pond.

The best part was realizing that my new strategy worked even if the waters around me continued to swirl. When I played duck, what changed was my perspective. It enabled me to feel safe... protected...even serene.

What about you?

- How do you react when you're confronted with the stressors of life? Do you react—or overreact? Do you allow them to affect you for hours or even days? Or do you have a coping strategy?

- Write about a recent circumstance in which you allowed your feathers to get ruffled. How might the situation have played out differently if you had let the situation roll off your back?

- Most of us, no matter what our spiritual or religious background, have heard the 23rd Psalm, which mentions that, in the valley of the shadow of death, our heads will be anointed with oil. Imagine that this anointing is God's love being poured all over your heart, mind and body, creating a soothing protective coating. Now write down a few thoughts about how that image changes how you feel.

Of a weary
heart longing
to be free

Adrenaline Detox

*"Sometimes the most urgent and vital thing you
can possibly do is take a complete rest."*
– Ashleigh Brilliant

One summer day when I was about 10 years old, I decided
to climb a tree. A big tree!

Instead of settling for the lower branches, I decided
to go all the way to the tippy top. It was one of the tallest trees in
Cuyahoga Falls, Ohio, and I could see the whole city from my
lofty vantage point.

What a view! The rush of adrenaline was incredible.

However, my euphoria shattered abruptly when my mom saw
me and freaked out at the danger I had put myself in. You see, the
branches at the top were pretty thin and brittle. But I was so caught

up in the thrill and emotion that I had hardly noticed. So there I was, clinging to fragile branches that seemed a mile off the ground, while my mom stood at the base of the tree threatening to tan my hide if I didn't come down that instant.

I was stuck. And suddenly the adrenaline that had propelled me to the top was gone; it was no help to me at all. All I could do was crawl back down, branch by fragile branch, terrified the whole way.

I wish I could say that was the last of my adrenaline-induced adventures, but it wasn't. Somehow, in that moment at the top of the tree, being scared out of my wits became my idea of a good time. Rather than sitting at home and being bored, I learned to love living on the edge, facing challenges most people are happy to avoid.

You might say I'm an adrenaline addict.

The adrenal gland triggers the release of hormones like dopamine, which is the body's natural painkiller, and epinephrine. These hormones also give our muscles the temporary boost to perform at peak strength during the well-known "fight or flight" response to danger or stress. The problem is that the body wasn't intended to remain in that heightened state indefinitely, which is exactly what has happened to some of us in today's society.

The rush of adrenaline is exhilarating, but as they say, "What goes up, must come down." When my doctor told me several years ago that I was suffering from adrenal exhaustion, I was shocked, though I guess I shouldn't have been. I thought I could live on adrenaline forever.

As a nurse, I've seen patients in this same state, some of them so exhausted from running so hard for so long that they could no longer drag themselves out of bed.

Addiction to adrenaline is not a healthy way to live, either physically or emotionally. Some people view their roller-coaster existence as normal, a typical reaction to the way we all seem to live in constant motion and under continuous stress. Some people pride themselves on living in hyper-drive. Some of us only feel alive when we're experiencing the rush that comes with overexerting our adrenal glands. Everything else feels flat, less alive.

That's where joy comes in.

One of the ways I've learned to live without my adrenaline fix is to focus not on being productive, but on making a contribution— primarily to the well-being of others. When I live in the moment, I find a deep, abiding joy that has nothing to do with what's happening on the outside.

This is a "rush" that has nothing to do with our adrenal glands. It's the lift that lasts—and it can begin in your life right now.

What about you?

- Do you feel more alive during times of stress, even negative stress? How much of your everyday life is spent in highly stressful circumstances? What does it take for you to "come down" from this stress?

- Journal about some strategies for walking on "level ground" and reducing the adrenaline effect in your life.

- Write about a time when you experienced something like true joy. What happened? What did it feel like? How often do you recall the experience?

From the pain and desperation that hovered over me

Radical Sabbatical

"My candle burns at both ends;
it will not last the night."
– Edna St. Vincent Millay

I f you had a whole day to do whatever you wanted, what would you do? I'm talking about a day when you don't have to worry about meeting deadlines at the office, catching up on housework, cooking dinner, paying bills, driving the kids to soccer practice, or checking e-mails from work. A day when you have no responsibilities at all—zip, zero, nada.

Sound pretty radical? Absolutely. But it also could be life-changing!

Even as a young girl, my daughter Abbie was hard-working and project-oriented. Although she loved spending time with friends and family, sometimes she'd simply had enough. Deciding that she needed some "Abbie time," she would light some candles, take a bubble bath, and then hide out in her room for a day or two. She would hang a big sign on her bedroom door:

ON A PERSONAL RETREAT
Please Do Not Disturb!

Abbie always came away from such times reinvigorated and full of fresh creativity and passion for life. This was quite an example for her hyperactive, Mrs. Fix-It mom.

As a wellness nurse, I've always been great at preaching to others that leisure, rest, recreation, and play are crucial to their physical and emotional health. But I'll admit, this is hard for me, and I've often found myself being quite a hypocrite.

During the rare moments of life when I find myself with nothing to do, a little voice tends to pop up in my brain, saying, "Don't just sit there idly. Get busy and DO something!" At those frequent moments, the people close to me sometimes have to remind me that even GOD took time to rest. Shouldn't we?

The problem for women can be that, no matter what else we do with our lives and our time and our talent, our home is always our place of work. We may have an office somewhere else, but when we're home, we're on duty. So most of us have to get away from home for our radical sabbaticals.

I remember one of my most rejuvenating sabbaticals, at a place called the Well of Mercy, a simple retreat center run by the Sisters of Mercy. Although I took my books, my journal, and my guitar, I spent the first three days simply *being*. I walked in nature, I ate healthy food prepared for me, I relaxed, I got in touch with my soul.

After I had emptied myself of all of the world's busyness, I turned to other things that fuel me, like reading and music. I spent time working on this book.

I hope you can periodically spend a few days at a mountain retreat center or even just follow Abbie's example and hang a "Do Not Disturb" sign on your bedroom or office door. Better yet, find a place where you can experience the kind of solitude and quiet I found at the Well of Mercy.

If that's not feasible right now, how about taking some baby steps? You can take a long walk in the woods, hike to the top of a nearby mountain, spend half a day browsing through books at your favorite bookstore, or take a few hours at the park to sit, walk, meditate, read, write…or better yet, just be.

Your time away from the hustle and bustle of life will allow you to unwind, unclog your brain, and regain your sense of vision and purpose. You'll be able to connect again with God and rediscover the unique design for your life. Do something that rests your spirit and feeds your soul!

What about you?

- Take a few minutes to write down what you would do on a perfect "radical sabbatical."

- Now get out your calendar and figure out when you can block out some time to make this happen. You may need to also explain to your spouse, kids, staff or employer why this is vitally important to you!

- Until the date for your radical sabbatical rolls around, why not commit to 15 minutes a day that is sacred time for you? Close the door, turn off the phone, do whatever you have to do to avoid distractions. Then, just be. Don't read. Don't text. Don't delete emails you're never going to open anyway. Don't even journal. Listen to music. Close your eyes. Take a nap. Meditate. Practice the Child's pose or the Corpse yoga posture. It's a lot more fun than it sounds! Or...

- Make a weekly or monthly commitment to doing something you've always wanted to do, but have put off doing because of that tired, old "no time" excuse. Take a painting class, learn how to swim, write a poem or three, practice those dance moves you haven't used since college, audition for a part in a local theater group, volunteer at the Humane Society, plan a Girls' Night Out to share fun and meaningful conversation with the most incredible women you know.

And I now can
move on to a
better place

Filling the Empty Nest

*"I don't want to get to the end of my life
and find that I lived just the length of it.
I want to have lived the width of it as well."*
– *Diane Ackerman*

My three kids are grown and gone, off to college, with careers and lives of their own.

When our nests are officially empty, we're happy and we're sad. The house feels different—too quiet, sometimes. We feel different—a bit hollow, after decades of filling our days and our hearts and our heads with raising children.

A wonderful season of our lives is over. It is time for us to give ourselves some of the attention we reserved for others. Some of us have no idea how to do that.

For me, this has become a time for discovering what I want to do with this important second half of my life. I finally got my own computer and my own bank account, after decades of sharing everything. It was scary for me and, I'll admit, not entirely welcomed by my husband. Sometimes women who have been so defined by our motherhood must change our lives so much that our growth and change can be alarming even to the best of husbands.

But we cannot waste this season—this season when our wisdom ripens, our minds and bodies can rest, and our souls can blossom.

It may mean adjustment for all those who love us—our husband, children, siblings, parents, and sometimes even our friends. But if we are not strong enough to take a stand for ourselves within our close relationships, how can we be strong enough to take a stand for ourselves with coworkers or strangers?

What about you?

- What will you harvest in the current season of your life?
- What seeds will you plant in this season of your life?
- In what relationships will you need to take a stand for fully experiencing this season of your life?

The tears dried
from my eyes

Fixing the Unfixable

"Never let a problem to be solved become more important than the person to be loved."
– Barbara Johnson

In the car on the way home from the gym, I was listening to a home improvement show. A woman called the radio station, wanting to know how to caulk her bathtub. She told the host of the program that her husband wasn't much of a handyman, so she was going to become "Mrs. Fix-It."

A flash of insight struck me when she called herself "Mrs. Fix-It." I thought to myself, *Wow! I've always tried to be a Mrs. Fix-It, too — just in a different way.*

I'm a strategizer. I've always loved to problem-solve, analyze, and figure things out. It's how I'm wired. As I constantly search for ways to make things better for myself and others, my mind finds it hard to shut down. I see problems everywhere, and I want to fix them all!

It can be a gift. It can also be a curse.

As you can imagine (or, as you may have experienced for yourself), being a Mrs. Fix-It is an exhausting job. There is never a shortage of situations that require help. And the busier I get trying to fix them, the more they seem to multiply. Like some sort of sadistic video game, no sooner do I shoot down one problem, when ten more appear.

Having been a Mrs. Fix-It for many years, I know it isn't easy to change. Fixing things—or believing we're fixing them—is addictive. I've gained a smug satisfaction at times from being able to point out all the seemingly insurmountable problems I've personally resolved. My whole self-image can get wrapped up in my ability to fix the unfixable.

Some things simply can't be fixed by human effort, no matter how noble the effort. The world is woefully imperfect. This is hard for fix-it people like me to accept. We'd like to believe we can fix anything we set our minds to.

Even more worrisome, I sometimes want to believe that if I don't solve the problem, it might never get fixed!

I've had to face a hard reality: If I could fix and control everything, I would be God! Instead, I've learned the hard way that when I try to fix the unfixable, I usually manage to just make things worse.

So today, I'm working on alternatives to being a fix-it person. I'm learning to let go. Relax. Be still. Stop striving as if the well-being of everyone I love and everything I encounter depends solely on me. I'm even finding out that when I don't try to run the world, the people I love are perfectly capable of running their own lives and solving their own dilemmas.

What about you?

- Make a list of some troubling areas of your life you are frequently tempted to "fix"—especially things that can't be fixed by human effort.

- Think about the times when you're tempted to go into "fix-it" mode. What are you feeling that you don't want to feel?

- What can you do instead of going into "fix-it" mode?

- Journal about a time in your life when you stepped in to "fix" something and ended up making things worse by offending someone or derailing someone else's solution.

A smile now
on my face

The Secret
of Serenity

"When we sip tea, we are on our way to serenity."
– Alexandra Stoddard

S erenity is not my default state of mind. On a scale of one to ten, there are times I would probably score a negative five! But I'm learning that worry today won't make tomorrow any better. In fact, it doesn't help much today either, and it certainly doesn't change a single thing that happened yesterday.

Most of us have heard Reinhold Niebuhr's Serenity Prayer: "God, grant me the serenity to accept the things I cannot change, courage to change the things I can, and wisdom to know the difference."

I have found myself reciting the Serenity Prayer many times during my life, particularly when encountering difficult circumstances that were out of my control to change. At times like that, it was easy to feel helpless and hopeless, frustrated that I could do nothing to alter the situation. Such times can be hard on anyone, but they are especially exasperating to someone who, as I've already confessed, wants to fix everything!

Here's another exasperating thing: Getting to serenity isn't about something I **do**, it's about changing the way I **think**.

The first step, according to the Serenity Prayer, is to stop knocking my head against a brick wall trying to change things I can't change. Instead, I have to accept those things I can't change. That doesn't mean I have to like them…or approve of them…it just means I have to accept that this is the way things are. So one way to look at this is that, once I've accepted that there are a lot of things I can't fix, I'm one-third of my way to serenity!

The second step is something I can do: I change the things I can change.

The third step in the prayer, and really a big fork in the road on the way to serenity, is to be able to **recognize the difference** between the things I can change and the things I cannot change.

I've learned that the only things I can really change are my own thoughts and my own actions. Or, another way of looking at it is to realize that I may not be able to change circumstances or other people, but I can change how I **react** to those circumstances or those people's actions.

In the children's book, *The Worry Tree*, worry is described as a tomato plant that gets so much attention that it sprouts and shoots out of control. It produces more tomatoes than anyone knows what to do with. Worry—or any other negative emotion—can be a lot like an out-of-control tomato plant. The more we feed and water it, the bigger it gets.

In *The Worry Tree*, children are encouraged to create a worry box in which to deposit their anxieties. Then, once a day, they open their worry box and share its contents with a trusted adult, who can tell them how to handle each concern in the box. For me, the Serenity Prayer is like a personal worry box, helping me figure out what to do with my fear or anxiety or worry.

One reason the Serenity Prayer is so effective is that it brings me back to a realization that I'm a mere mortal. It reminds me that it is the height of arrogance to think I will be able to change all of life's most challenging circumstances by my own human efforts.

If you are a praying person, you know the power of opening your worry box to discuss its contents with One who is all-powerful.

Not a praying person yet? The Serenity Prayer can be a comfortable and powerful starting point. Or it might help to simply write your worries and concerns on a list or in a journal. Just get it off your chest and onto paper. This isn't magic, but it often can help make you feel less overwhelmed.

Embrace the freedom that serenity brings. Yes, bad things will happen sometimes. Sickness, car wrecks, lost jobs, tornadoes, broken relationships, and even our children's disappointments can seem almost unbearable. They remain a part of life, even though we want to believe we can *surely* change them if we're determined enough. Experiencing bad things goes with the territory, and sometimes we simply don't understand why we go through the things we do.

But as Reinhold Niebuhr concludes: "The final wisdom of life requires not the annulment of incongruity but the achievement of serenity within and above it." Questions may remain, but serenity enables us to rise above life's incongruities.

What about you?

- In your journal, make two separate lists. In the first list, write down things you cannot change, but simply must accept. In the second list, write down things you believe you personally can change by the proper desire, effort and perseverance. Pay special attention to the second list, making sure you aren't including situations that really aren't yours to change.

- Talk to someone wise about your two lists—not someone you know will agree with you no matter what, but someone you can rely on to help you gain clear perspective. Get that person's input.

- Now place the items on the first list in your own version of a worry box, or visualize handing over your list to God.

- For items on the second list, create a basic action plan of steps you can take to bring about progress.

My tired soul is
finally at rest

Recovering Your Lost Song

"A bird doesn't sing because it has an answer,
it sings because it has a song."
– Maya Angelou

When we moved from Ohio to Florida, I realized after a few days that my blue Parakeet was being awfully quiet. Tweety had always been a joyful chirper while we lived in Ohio—but now it seemed he had lost his song. It appeared that the trauma of moving across the country and adjusting to a new climate was more than he could bear. When days passed without a song from Tweety, I became concerned that he might even die from the strain of our move.

For a whole month, Tweety's silence continued, to the point that I wondered if he would ever be the same again.

Then, as suddenly as it had disappeared, Tweety's song returned about a month after our move. What a relief to hear his happy chirping fill our kitchen once again.

Birds aren't the only creatures that can lose their song—people can, too! In fact, although I love to write and sing new songs, I find that my internal happy song grows right out of the experiences that initially silenced the song in my soul.

Most of my songs have grown out of hurt and broken places in my life; the healing comes after the fact, at least partly because I hear from others that my songs bring them comfort or hope.

Although my music seems to come naturally, I'm not prolific and I'm not trained. I can't read music, and my ability to play the guitar is limited. So when I wake in the middle of the night with music and lyrics in my head—in my heart, really—the only thing I can do is sing what I hear and rely on someone else to transcribe the notes.

That's the way it is sometimes in recovering our lost songs. We have to sing what's in there, even if we need help making sense of it in the beginning.

Like Tweety, we've all experienced traumatic events that temporarily rob us of our joy and peace. Illness, betrayal, death, loss of all kinds. Amid such traumas, it can seem that our song might be gone forever.

Also like Tweety, we need to cultivate resilience. And resilience rises out of our hope that whatever the trauma, we will recover our song. Or learn a completely new one.

Resilience is the positive capacity of people to cope with stress, catastrophe, adversity, and trauma. Those who are resilient can more quickly regain their equilibrium and spring back to sanity if they're temporarily thrown off-kilter by the storms of life.

Al Siebert writes of this in *The Resiliency Advantage*:

Highly resilient people are flexible, adapt to new circumstances quickly, and thrive in constant change. Most important, they expect to bounce back and feel confident that they will. They have a knack for creating good luck out of circumstances that many others see as bad luck. They are adept at seeing things from another person's point of view.

Does this definition of resilience describe you? Are you able to maintain your flexibility when adapting to change or bouncing back from adversity? Or do you sometimes feel like a brittle rubber band that's on the verge of snapping if it is stretched any farther?

Sometimes our cries for restoration will be answered immediately and directly. Other times, restoration will be a process—involving time, study, journaling, prayer, meditation, counseling, listening to our wise friends and mentors, or just basking in the sweet words of friends and loved ones to resurrect our joy. Plato described this well: "Every heart sings a song, incomplete, until another heart whispers back. Those who wish to sing always find a song. At the touch of a lover, everyone becomes a poet."

What about you?

- Take a few minutes to review your life, and create a rough graph of how your joy has gone up or down throughout the years. Were there times when you, like Tweety, "lost your song" for a while? If so, journal about how you got your song back.

- If you still feel traumatized by some painful experience or failure in your life, how can you help yourself trust that the process of restoration will work for you, too?

- What does it mean to you to "lose your song"? What joyful expressions of your unique self seem to wither and die when you are sad, traumatized, exhausted, or discouraged? What part of you can feel, at times, as if it will be gone forever, never to be restored?

I look with
expectation
to days that
lie ahead

The Rules
of the ICU

*"The great omission in American life is solitude...
that zone of time and space, free from the outside pressures,
which is the incubator of the spirit."*
– Marya Mannes

Hospital Intensive Care Units often have a "No Visitors" policy. Sometimes this is annoying to friends and relatives who are denied access, but as a nurse I understand the reasons for such rules.

A person who is critically sick or injured often needs plenty of peace and quiet in order to get better. They are fragile physically, and often emotionally as well. Insensitive to this situation, some visitors are like bulls in a china shop—full of energy and emotion, but unable to sit still and be quiet. At times I've even seen visitors forget that it can literally be lifesaving for a doctor or nurse to have access to the patient without having to dodge a panicked or well-meaning loved one.

Sometimes we ourselves are in the "emotional ICU." Other times, we must respect the privacy of others who are in this condition.

Solitude feels uncomfortable in our always-connected society, but it can bring healing and spiritual depth to our lives. During the fragile times in our lives, we need to find a safe, peaceful place to heal and regain lost strength. The need for solitude as a way to connect spiritually is an indispensable part of the authentic life.

If you are currently in the emotional ICU, make the most of it. You aren't meant to spend the rest of your life in the ICU—it is only temporary. Take this opportunity to heal and restore and get back on your feet.

What about you?

- When you are in need of healing, are you more prone to isolate yourself to seek comfort in solitude, or do you usually seek out the companionship of other people as part of the healing process?

- When you turn to solitude, how do you use it? Do you meditate, journal, get back to nature, take time to reflect on the circumstances that may have brought you into emotional ICU? Or do you tend to isolate for the sake of hiding from others, licking your wounds, building emotional walls to protect yourself?

- When friends or loved ones experience traumatic circumstances, how do you assure that you're being sensitive to the rules of their personal ICU?

- Sometimes we wind up in an emotional ICU because we haven't taken precautions against toxic people. Journal about your own tendency to become weak or infected by toxic relationships. How might you use some time in ICU to recover and build up your immunity to toxic relationships?

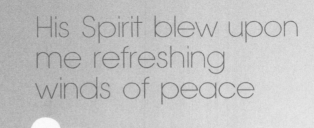

His Spirit blew upon
me refreshing
winds of peace

Playing Whac-a-Mole

"Perfectionism is self-abuse of the highest order."
– Anne Wilson Schaef

If personal effort could produce perfection, I would've been there a long time ago.

Maybe you can identify with that. Women way too often believe we need to be perfection times ten.

I've come to the painful realization that even if I conquer one of the habits or traits that keep me from perfection, there's always another staring me in the face. It's like the Whac-a-Mole game at an archade, where you use a mallet to smash the moles that keep popping out. The more smashing you do, the faster the moles seem to pop up! The pace accelerates and you realize there's no way to smash them all.

The road to perfection is not only uphill—it's unending! The closer I get to what I once thought was perfection, the more I realize how thoroughly imperfect I am.

So what's a perfectionist to do about this impossible mission?

First, it is important to remember perfection does not exist here in this life. We're not perfect and we're not meant to be. A friend who is also a spiritual director tells me we are all perfectly human, and that translates into being perfectly imperfect.

Second, the apparent flawlessness you see in others is just an illusion. Everyone puts their best foot forward on Facebook and in their holiday letters. Even the celebrities on magazine covers don't look that way without a lot of airbrushing and Photoshopping.

Can you imagine what you would think of Mrs. Perfect down the street if her Facebook status updates mentioned her marital and financial problems? Or her last health report? Or the fact that nobody mentioned her skirt was tucked into the back of her pantyhose before she exited the ladies room at the country club? Despite appearances, you can be sure her life is far from perfect.

Never forget that perfection is unattainable.

That doesn't mean that we can't take on some of the things that trouble us about ourselves. I know a few of us touch up those gray roots from time to time and there's nothing wrong with that. But when we take our desire to improve ourselves to an extreme, we can wear ourselves out with our game of personal Whac-a-Mole.

What is it about yourself that you would like to see changed? Is it something in your personality? An unruly tongue? An undisciplined thought life? Difficulty getting along with others? Pinpoint the issues that cause the most pain or problems in your life, as well as the ones you can realistically control. Then seek out a counselor or life coach to help you tackle the issues you're struggling with. If that seems a bit too expensive for your current budget, perhaps you can find a pastor or a wise friend who can point you to your greatest potential. Or join our online health and well-being community, MaryBuchan.com, where you'll find plenty of support and encouragement and can sign up for a free newsletter.

But quit wearing yourself out by trying to remedy your imperfections through Whac-a-Mole. Smashing endless moles may lead to perspiration, but certainly not perfection.

What about you?

- Instead of focusing on the things that you want to change, use your journal today to focus on what's great about you. What are your best character traits? What if the best way to improve yourself is to build on those strengths instead of nitpicking about all the ways you aren't perfect?

- Ask your friends what your strengths are. Listen. Write down what they say.

- Imagine that you are encouraging a child you dearly love to change her behaviors. Now talk to yourself about the behaviors you want to change—and talk to yourself exactly the way you would talk to that child.

The old has blown
away, the new has
been released

When You Feel Like You're Under It, Get Over It

"Let me come in where you are weeping, friend, and let me take your hand. I who have known a sorrow such as yours can understand."
— *Grace Noll Crowell*

I was shocked the Sunday morning an arrogant young preacher presented his views on counseling.

"So, you want to know what I think of counseling?" he asked with a cocky flair. "Here's the only real counsel you will ever need: *'Get over it!'"*

The congregation laughed uneasily, not knowing how seriously to take his remarks. Some people seemed to think he had made a great point. Perhaps they were the ones who had already "gotten over it," and who felt everyone else should be "over it" by now, too.

Yet some of us in the congregation that day felt like we were drowning, sinking for the third time while a condescending young lifeguard stood at the edge of the pool, shouting, "Swim, you wimps! Swim!"

If you don't know how to swim, all the exhortations in the world will be of no help. Some of us had no clue how to get over it, and at times we felt too "under it" to even make an effort.

Most of the things we have to "get over" didn't happen the day before yesterday or even last year. Most of the things we have to "get over" started early, which means the roots of those emotions and memories go deep. Getting over the fact that my mother, who suffered from bi-polar disorder, was not perfect required something more than just deciding I was over it. For me, it required realizing what my mother had to "get over"—and what **her** mother had to "get over."

After my mother died last year, I stood at her grave and, for the first time in a long time, I thought of the night my mom's mother died.

I was 12 years old at the time. In the middle of the night, Mother climbed into my twin bed with me, wrapped her arms around me and whispered, "My mother just died."

Mom perceived that my Grandma Francis was a difficult alcoholic. She'd been known to chase my mom with a knife when she was too inebriated to realize what she was doing. The night she died, she was in a hospital, in an alcoholic coma. As my mother left the hospital for the night, she turned back to Grandma Francis and whispered, "Mother, I love you."

Before she turned back to the door, my mother saw her mother, deep in her coma, raise a hand.

To Mother, it felt like an acknowledgment and an affirmation of something Grandma Francis had never been able to say aloud. Mother took that lifted hand as a response: I love you, too.

As I stood at Mother's grave, I realized that she had done the best she could, having grown up in a harsh environment where she received no nurturing. And no doubt, Grandma Francis had experienced her full share of the harshness of life.

They had both done the best they could.

And in that moment, I got over it.

But I couldn't "get over it" just because someone told me to. Not even when that someone was a preacher.

Getting over it is easier said than done. Sometimes we get buried under a pile of unfortunate circumstances: divorce, estranged children, death of loved ones, abusive relationships, loss of a job, health problems, false accusations, or the death of our dreams.

While some things we need to get over are the result of our own wrong decisions, often we find ourselves the victim of events that weren't our fault at all.

So what **can** we do to truly get over the difficult events of life?

Cancel the Pity Party: Even though we have all been a victim at one time or another, we first need to actively let go of any victim mentality. That means ruthlessly casting off any self-pity, and refusing to wallow in our victimhood. It is no sin to be "under it" at one time or another—but it helps nothing to stay there.

Unburden: Perhaps you'll need to unburden your heart to a trusted friend or counselor. What an extraordinary blessing it is to find a safe, gracious, constructive environment where you can express your true feelings.

Wail it Out: If you're a person who prays, don't hesitate to speak up in those prayers about how you really feel. This isn't the time for a sweet and shallow "Now I lay me down to sleep" prayer. It's okay to get real about your loneliness or anger or depression. I've come to believe that it's okay to let God know if we disagree with how the universe is being run. After all, even the saints in the Bible had as many complaints as they did praises. One of our modern-day saints, Mother Teresa, is known for questioning the harshness of the world.

Why would saints struggle to accept the state of the world? Because in order to "get over" what we've been under, we need to be utterly honest about our circumstances, our feelings, and our needs. So cry if you need to—a good, soul-cleansing cry!

Take a look at this verse from Psalm 34, written by King David following some pretty straightforward grumbling: *"You turned my wailing into dancing; you removed my sackcloth and clothed me with joy."*

That says to me that in order to get over it, we must get real about our wailing and our grieving. We can't just snap our fingers and get over it. We must go deep within and beyond ourselves to a higher power.

What about you?

- Make a list of some of the things in your life that you need to "get over." Have you held onto any of them too long?

- Write your own psalm of wailing and grieving as a first step in turning things over to God.

- Get honest in your journal about people you blame for the things that have hurt you. Work on letting go of any resentment and blame.

- Now journal about anything good that has flowed out of those things in your life that you'd like to "get over"—any unexpected blessings or outcomes that you wouldn't change now, even if you could. Recognize the gifts. Use them to start a gratitude list. Even better, create a gratitude book to support your personal growth.

I will never be
the same since
His Spirit blew
upon me

Twisted Mirrors

*"You can fool yourself, you know.
You'd think it's impossible, but it turns out
it's the easiest thing of all."*
– Jodi Picoult

I will never forget the day I went to the Ohio State Fair and visited the House of Mirrors. Although I was skinny as a rail, I looked quite fat in some of the mirrors. Meanwhile, other mirrors made my not-as-thin friends look super thin.

Needless to say, everyone looked strange in the House of Mirrors, and I guess that was its appeal. Even though we could recognize ourselves in the distorted mirrors, they clearly weren't providing an accurate picture of what we really looked like.

Many people live their entire lives in a House of Mirrors. They see themselves in the twisted reflections they receive from those around them.

- They're not fat...but they *see themselves* as too fat.
- They're not skinny...but they *see themselves* as too skinny.
- They're not stupid...but they *see themselves* as stupid.
- They're not a failure...but they *see themselves* as a failure.
- They're not unloved...but they *see themselves* as unlovable.

It might be fun visiting the House of Mirrors at an amusement park or state fair, but it sure isn't fun to live your life there.

When I say I was skinny growing up, I mean I was very skinny. My classmates called me "bird legs" and other unflattering names. I felt like an ugly duckling, and these feelings were hard to shake even when I grew up. It was a long time before I could look at myself and see a swan. Even well into adulthood, I looked at pictures of that little girl and all I could see was how skinny and ugly she looked through the twisted mirror I carried around in my head.

When we embrace the truth about ourselves, we can escape the House of Mirrors!

If we don't know who we are, there are plenty of people ready to define us. Sadly, when we allow ourselves to be defined by distorted mirrors, we forfeit our true identities. When we don't have a clear sense of our own identity and mission, other people supply us with theirs. Instead of finding our unique personalities and calling, we actually distort ourselves—twist ourselves—into becoming a reflection of them, their needs and wants, their dreams.

As Oprah Winfrey wisely observed, "It isn't until you come to a spiritual understanding of who you are—not necessarily a religious feeling, but deep down, the spirit within—that you can begin to take control." How powerful and true.

Women owe it to themselves to ditch our distorted mirrors and see ourselves as we were really intended to be.

What about you?

- Describe some distorted ways you've tended to see yourself in the past. Where did these distorted images originate? Have you really destroyed your twisted mirrors, or do you sometimes sneak a peek at them?

- Have you taken an honest look at the people around you and the influences and the mirrors they hold up to you? How many of those mirrors are distorted?

- What wise self-talk can you use when you find yourself staring into a twisted mirror?

- Think about the women you influence, including coworkers, the people you manage at work, people you mentor professionally, neighborhood friends, and even your nieces or daughters or granddaughters. Are you holding up any distorted mirrors for them? How can you encourage them to wipe their true mirrors clean and see themselves as they really are?

I can see a
window opening

Pick Out a New Wardrobe

"I love new clothes. If everyone could just wear new clothes everyday, I reckon depression wouldn't exist anymore."

– Sophie Kinsella

When I was a young bride, I dressed with such modesty that I could have been mistaken for a Mennonite. High collars, drab colors, no make-up or jewelry. And I might as well have taken a vow of poverty like the Franciscans in my own Catholic faith—I bought most of those drab clothes from Goodwill.

Things have changed. I've finally taken off my self-effacing timidity and learned to put on some confidence. I still don't wear much make-up or jewelry, but I want some color in my wardrobe. Over the years, I've worked hard to keep my body fit, so I want my clothes to be flattering.

And I admit it—I love to shop for new clothes. Just ask my family.

Our clothes reveal a lot about us. They let the world know what we value—comfort or style or professionalism or the need to be considered attractive. They tell the world a lot about our mood and our attitude toward life—are we serious or playful or easygoing or cheerful?

Our actions are another kind of clothing. When we are kind, we clothe ourselves in graciousness, which is a beautiful garment. When we're impatient or rude, we're wearing an outfit that tells the world that what's beneath the surface may not be very attractive.

Every day, we make choices about how we'll handle situations— good and bad—that come our way. Will we respond with grace? Will we growl at the world around us?

When a driver cuts in front of us on the freeway, and anger wells up within us...we can take off our anger and put on the garment of patience.

When we see a friend being honored, and jealousy rises in our hearts...we can take off jealousy and put on love.

When we're tempted to gossip or use our words to tear people down...we can take off our ugly words and wear the language of kindness or encouragement.

When we feel like grumbling or giving in to despair...we can exchange our negativity for a garment of gratitude.

Of course, trading in the behaviors and attitudes that we're comfortable wearing isn't as easy as taking last year's shoes to Goodwill and then shopping at Macy's for this year's style. It takes a conscious effort to lay aside our negative or destructive actions and attitudes and replace them with something that reflects kindness and love.

Haven't we worn the old, drab garments long enough? Isn't it time to go shopping?

What about you?

- What's hanging in your emotional closet that you've outgrown? What old behaviors do you put on every day, even though the fabric is faded or the soles are worn through? What just doesn't fit any longer?

- Wear something new every day this week and journal about how that makes you feel.

A second wind,
the fragrance
of new life

When It's Storming, Look Up

"I am not afraid of storms
for I am learning how to sail my ship."
— *Louisa May Alcott*

Tornadoes hardly ever strike Myrtle Beach, South Carolina. So that was the last thing we expected when we decided to spend the Fourth of July weekend there in 2001, along with nearly 400,000 other unsuspecting vacationers.

My 8-year-old son, Ben, was on the beach with neighbor friends who were vacationing with us. Feeling safe in the family-friendly atmosphere, we lost sight of the boys. By the time we saw the lightning, the boys were out of sight.

Afternoon thunderstorms are commonplace at the beach. *No big deal*, we thought.

Then the sky became eerily gray. The wind intensified. Dust and debris began to swirl all around us. Beach chairs spun in the air. Lifeguards quickly evacuated the beach.

Still no sign of Ben or his friends.

Meanwhile, this vicious funnel of destruction ravaged a two-mile path along the beach, with winds up to 157 miles an hour, knocking over buses and utility poles, damaging roofs, and blowing out windows in buildings and vehicles.

Just as the danger reached its pinnacle, lifeguards arrived in their pickup truck with Ben's friends—but without Ben. When I learned the boys had been separated, I feared the worst.

I discovered later that Ben had found his way back to our room, completely unharmed. He had taken cover right before the tornado reached its destructive climax. His safety seemed a miracle, to say the least.

I had been on the fringe of powerful storms before, but this time my family was in the epicenter. The worst damage occurred at the Myrtle Beach Pavilion, right where we had been enjoying our peaceful vacation. About 400,000 homes were left without power. Our minivan was totaled by the high winds and debris.

None of that mattered once it was clear that everyone was safe and unharmed.

This event taught me some important lessons about the storms of life. First, storms can be scary, particularly when they come out of nowhere, when we least expect them. Without warning, blue skies and sunny days can be replaced by dark clouds and torrential rains. Second, storms have a way of showing us what's really important. As the Myrtle Beach tornado brought its swirling destruction my way, I realized our van and our belongings were of little value in comparison to the safety of my son.

And just as the water spouts in the Atlantic converged that holiday week in Myrtle Beach, the storms of life often come at us from all directions, making it almost impossible to protect ourselves.

Ask Lisa Beamer, who was pregnant with her third child when her husband Todd died aboard United Flight 93, which crashed a few months after our holiday weekend, on September 11, 2001. Amid her grief, she had the courage to look above her circumstances to the Source of her faith, which she relied on to restore her hope.

Elisabeth Elliot can tell you all about storms, too. After waiting five years to marry her missionary husband, Jim, she received the news that he'd been brutally murdered by the tribesmen he had been trying to help. After grieving and ultimately remarrying, her second husband died, too. How did she find the strength to go on? She, too, leaned on her faith for comfort and the reassurance that her experiences had a purpose greater than her individual life.

Lisa Beamer and Elisabeth Elliot are not superheroes. They faced human feelings and emotions just like us. Yet they learned to transcend their difficult circumstances—to live above them—by searching for and focusing on a higher purpose.

So when the storms of life converge on you from every side, look beyond yourself. Look up, to a higher purpose.

What about you?

- Journal about a time when a sudden storm caught you by surprise. How did you respond? How did you gather your courage to survive the storm?

- Life's storms can help us see what is truly important in our lives. If you faced a serious tornado, hurricane, flood, earthquake, or other natural disaster, what would you go to any lengths to keep safe?

- Who in your life would you turn to for help if the winds were converging from every direction? Journal about why you would make this choice.

Refreshing
oxygen

Holding On, Letting Go, and Moving On

"Leap, and the net will appear."
– Julie Cameron

I was in the second grade when Mom and Dad took us to the skating rink. It was scary, watching all those bigger kids whiz by on their roller skates, but I really wanted to be one of them.

My dad held my hand tightly as we skated together around the rink. I still remember the energy I felt radiate from his hand to mine—it made me feel warm and protected. I knew if I fell, he would pick me up. Confident that I was taken care of, it wasn't long before I let go of his hand and skated by myself. I became a good skater.

The scene was much the same as he took off my bike's training wheels and taught me how to ride on two wheels.

Both times, I was glad to have my dad's steady hand to get me started. There was a time to hang on, but if I really wanted to get somewhere, eventually I had to let go.

I meet a lot of people who are still clutching some security blanket—clutching it so tightly, in fact, that they are nearly suffocating. When that happens, we stifle our own progress.

Several years ago, I found myself moving from Ohio to Florida, where my husband was starting an exciting new job in ministry and writing. Although we were both thrilled at the wonderful opportunity, the move created traumatic changes that seemed to rock my entire world.

I had lived in Ohio my entire life. So this move required leaving behind my parents, longtime friends, job, church, aunts and uncles, cousins—and a whole lot of precious memories. I felt as if I were leaving a piece of me behind in Ohio. As the airplane took off toward Orlando, tears streamed down my cheeks.

I always thought it sounded so glamorous to "follow your dreams," but now I was confronted with the stark reality of letting go in order for our family to move on. Would I be able to find my own dreams in this strange new world?

Life presents each of us with moments of decision and crossroads where we can either choose a new direction and move on, or cling to what we already have.

What is your decision? Are you willing to leave your comfort zone, letting go of people, places and things that would hold you back from living your best life? What security blankets might you have to give up in order to make room for new opportunities?

Although change isn't always easy, I've discovered that we don't need to fear the future, it's going to unfold and be there whether we are ready or not.

What about you?

- How would you respond today if life offered you the opportunity to hold onto everything you presently have (your career, resources, relationships, security, etc.), or venture in the direction of your most cherished dream?

- Journal about a time when you've lost something you treasured, only to realize later that it opened the door for one of life's great gifts.

- Journal about a time when you lost an opportunity because you wouldn't make a change. Have you regretted your decision? What would you do differently today?

- What part of your life are you entirely unwilling to give up today?

Past the veil of mystery, beyond the night

When It Hurts, Say 'Ouch'

*"The pain of an injury is over in seconds.
Everything that comes after is the pain of getting well."*
— *Tessa Dare*

I'll never forget the day little Danny Kasberg fell off the five-foot-high plastic slide in Sunday School class. He and some of the other three-year-olds were being rambunctious, the way three-year-olds can be. And before I could intervene, Danny fell flat on his back with a loud thud.

All eyes turned toward Danny. All of us, I think, expected him to scream out in pain or fear or both.

A bit stunned, Danny exclaimed, "Ouch!" Then he got up and went back to playing.

Yes, children can teach us some of our most profound lessons.

First, Danny said "Ouch!" As adults, most of us have learned too well how to hide our pain. Acknowledging that we're sick, in emotional pain, or struggling with our vulnerability can be seen as a weakness.

But young Danny hadn't yet learned to stuff his pain—he said, "Ouch!"

Although it was certainly appropriate for Danny to acknowledge that the fall hurt him, he had a decision to make at that point. As he lay on his back and looked around, he could see everyone staring at him. It would have been easy to milk the moment for some sympathy and attention. Yet Danny chose to get up and begin playing again.

What a contrast with the way many of us grownups react. Either we refuse to say "Ouch" and acknowledge our distress; or we choose to remain on the ground as long as we can, looking for as much sympathy as we can generate. Some of us go far beyond saying "Ouch"—we stay on the ground and indulge in self-pity.

When I was about Danny's age, I tripped on the neighbor's gravel driveway and cut my knees. At the sight of blood, I screamed like crazy and became combative toward my friends when they tried to help me. Finally, an adult neighbor carried me home, where my mom bandaged my wounds.

Was I injured? Yes. Did I overreact? Absolutely. Instead of merely saying "Ouch," I was so melodramatic that it would've been easy to assume I needed a hospital bed...or at least a few stitches!

Danny also avoided another favorite adult reaction to injury: He didn't look for somebody to blame. How easy it would have been to get into the tattle-tale mode and complain that the whole thing was "Johnny's fault." But while blame-shifting momentarily helps us save face, in the long run it does us no good.

Many people find their life unraveling because they haven't learned Danny's lessons. Some get stuck because they have never said "Ouch" and asked for healing. Others remain lying on the floor, refusing to get up and resume their lives again. And some stay stuck because they insist on blaming others rather than taking responsibility for their own mishaps.

The next time you find yourself falling on your back, remember that it's alright to say "Ouch." But don't forget to get back up and start playing again.

What about you?

- What's your inclination when you fall off life's sliding board? Do you say "Ouch" and keep playing? Do you howl about the pain until you've received enough sympathy to suit you? Do you blame somebody else? Hold a grudge? How does your particular reaction to being hurt make you feel? How do others react to your reactions?

- Do you have a few trustworthy people in your life who offer a safe place for you to say "Ouch" when you are really hurting?

I can see the
new horizon with
the dawning of
the light

Let Your Ducks Fall Where They May

"No one ever died from sleeping in an unmade bed."
— Erma Bombeck

I have a confession: My ducks are not all in a row.

And thank goodness I've reached the age where I can let the ducks fall where they may.

It wasn't always so. I'll never forget the dream a friend told me one day, years ago. In his dream, he saw me sitting at my kitchen table. Sitting across from me was Jesus, and we were in deep conversation. I sure wish my friend had been able to tell me about that conversation!

However, in his dream, something kept distracting me from my conversation with Jesus.

In the dream, a row of decorative wooden ducks was arranged in perfect order on a ledge next to the kitchen table. And while I was trying to give my full attention to the conversation, those ducks started falling over. Distracted, I stopped to put the ducks in their places again. But the ducks kept falling over and I kept turning my attention away from what was surely the most important conversation of my life—all because I was obsessed with keeping those ducks in a row!

I should be embarrassed to admit how accurate my friend's dream image was.

For years I was obsessed by the effort to get my ducks in order, only to have them quickly regress to their disorderly condition. As a mother of three young children, the Second Law of Thermodynamics was painfully evident: Things really do tend to go from a state of order to disorder!

Whether housework, laundry, cooking, relationships, or spiritual disciplines, it doesn't take long for things to fall into a state of disarray.

The answer is not just trying harder to maintain order. I've discovered that even ducks I've carefully put in order eventually fall down from time to time. Trying harder just leads to more frustration.

So what is the solution to this frustrating fact of life?

For me, the answer has been to remember that I was designed for excellence, not perfection.

Life is not perfect. Never has been, never will be. So never mind the order of my ducks. I need to focus instead on the unique expression of my own gifts and an understanding of my Creator's priorities for me. There will never be another person exactly like me or exactly like you. What a terrible thing it is to deprive the world of the gifts we were created to bring, simply because we were too busy trying to keep our ducks in a row!

Now is the time to think big, take risks, and live our dreams. It is time to express our gifts and talents. It is time to let all of our experiences and our accumulated wisdom come together in an expression of our best self, living the best life we were created to live.

What about you?

- List some of the ducks that fall down and distract you from what's really important in your life. Which ones are really more important than expressing your gifts or living your dreams? What is the worst possible outcome if you stop lining up all the ducks in your life?

- What dreams and desires have you postponed over the years by telling yourself that you don't have time?

- Is it possible that the ducks keep you from facing some other fear that is really behind your choice not to focus on your gifts and dreams? Name some possible fears and write about what would happen if you let them fall down with all those ducks.

- Journal about some of the ways that perfectionism holds you back.

A clean and
holy breeze,
flowing over me

Brain Washing

"I have learned from experience that the greater part of our happiness or misery depends on our dispositions and not on our circumstances."
– Martha Washington

My husband and I went to beautiful Jamaica for our honeymoon. One day as we were browsing through the marketplace, a friendly young man offered to give us a tour of Dunn's River Falls, one of the most famous tourist attractions in the area. The price he quoted seemed reasonable, so we took him up on his offer.

This enterprising young man took us and one other couple on an interesting route, past a woman washing her clothes…an old man taking a bath…and some vacant fields of sugar cane.

Soon we were at a small waterfall in a rather remote area of the rain forest.

"Here it is!" he proudly exclaimed as we came into view of a small waterfall. "Put your heads under the water, and get your brains washed!"

We discovered the following day that the real Dunn's River Falls was several miles away from the destination we'd been led to by our charming tour guide. He had completely hoodwinked us. Maybe his understanding of the nuances of the English language were better than we thought when he was encouraging us to have our brains washed.

Still, I've never forgotten our guide's exhortation to have our brains washed. That lasting imagery was worth the price of the tour.

Because we live in an unraveling world, our minds are subjected to many unhealthy influences—many are displayed via TV, radio, movies, newspapers, magazines, billboards, countless sources from the Internet. Our culture bombards us with negative messages and gruesome perspectives on life. Unless we make a commitment to having our "brains washed" on a daily basis, we will soon find our best selves engulfed by unhealthy world views.

So if we want to make progress in life, we may need to get our brains washed. A cluttered or muddied mind will not get us where we really want to go.

One of my spiritual guides would light a candle whenever I came to see her, reminding me that this was our time to be quiet, even if only for five minutes.

Sometimes I ask a clarifying question when I feel my mind becoming muddied: Is this thought true?

Another wonderful way to clear the mind is through exercise, which gives us a chance to reconnect our body, spirit, and mind.

What about you?

- In what ways is your mind polluted? Where do you regularly absorb negativism, ingratitude, violence, greed, envy, a warped self-image, dishonesty, and other types of "stinking thinking"? Identify some of the ways in which you need to wash your brain and fill it with a new perspective.

- What are some ways you can cleanse your mind on a regular basis? Meditation, prayer, mindful exercise, physical exercise, uplifting or encouraging reading, sabbaticals from media? Make a list of anything that occurs to you. Then develop a plan to set aside a specified time each day to cleanse your mind.

I'm free, I'm free,
His Spirit blew
upon me

Power Source

"There came a time when the risk to remain tight in the bud was more painful than the risk it took to blossom."

– Anais Nin

When your furnace quits working or your lights go out, the first thing to do is find your power box!

Every house has this nerve center of electrical power, a hub of circuit breakers or fuses through which all of your house's electricity must pass in order to do its job. If the circuit breakers shut down, there's no power in the house. When this central hub functions properly, it governs the use of power throughout your home, apportioning 15 amps of power where needed, 30 amps where appropriate, etc. Because if 60 amps of power is funneled where 15 amps is needed, an overloaded fuse could blow. And somewhere, something will shut down completely because its 60 amp power need isn't being met.

You were designed with your own power box—one overwhelming passion that fuels your life. It is meant to energize you and funnel power to your daily needs.

Your heart's power box represents the big dream or personal mission statement that should govern your life. It is the central hub through which every other activity or relationship should pass. It is the key to your health and success.

However, too many of us don't even realize that we have a power box in our hearts. We are so busy chasing material gain or energy-draining relationships that there's little energy or time left to discover or maintain our source of power. Then our circuit breakers shut down and block the flow of energy.

Like a house with a power failure, life gets cold and dark if our power box malfunctions. We search here and there in vain, trying to navigate a pitch-black room after the power goes out. Until we find and repair the power box, every other remedy will be in vain.

A friend of mine spent most of her professional life in the arts, until she hit the age of 50 and was going through a rocky period in her life. To gain economic stability, she took a job in a corporate setting. She had business cards and a title and she woke up early every weekday morning and drove to an office and put in her time and came home at the end of every weekday entirely depleted. When people asked the question we all seem to get—"What do you do?"—she found herself fumbling to answer a question that left her feeling like a fraud and a failure.

Then one day, a few months before she turned 60, she realized that she wasn't just getting closer to the end of her life chronologically. She realized that she had cut herself off from her power source and she was slowly but surely dying.

She left the job. She pitched out the business cards. She went back to her art. And one day someone asked her, "What do you do?"

She said, "I'm an artist."

Something inside her bloomed when she said that. And the person who asked the question said later, "You should see your face when you say, 'I'm an artist.'"

My friend had reconnected to her power source.

How long has it been since you felt truly alive? Since you felt a sincere love for life and a true passion for what you were doing? Maybe it's been so long ago that you've virtually given up hope of ever regaining your zest for life. But it's not too late to discover or rediscover what really fuels you, the true passion that feeds your power box.

Have you found your power box yet? If you have, then it should govern all of the smaller pursuits in your life. It should funnel resources and energy in proportion to how every part of your life fits into your central purpose for living.

What about you?

- What represents the central energy hub in your life? What pursuit or passion fuels everything you do?

- How do all the other activities in your life flow from that central power source? Do they connect?

- Have you bypassed your central energy hub in order to fuel a part of your life that demands more than its share of fuel? Where is this misdirection of energy showing up? What are you starving of the energy it needs in order to fill its true role in your best life?

Refreshing winds
of peace

Claim Your Strength

"Women are like teabags. We don't know
our true strength until we are in hot water!"
— *Eleanor Roosevelt*

O kay, maybe I'm strange, but I enjoy working out.
That doesn't mean there aren't times when the physical
challenge of it feels like more than I can handle.

One morning, in a very strenuous step aerobics class, I was
more tired than usual. The class was a little more than half over
and I was ready to give up. I told myself I simply wasn't strong
enough to continue. I was about to sneak out the back door when
the animated aerobics instructor called out to the class, "Come on,
don't give up now. You're strong!"

Could she read my mind? I wondered. Her unexpected words struck me as more than just the standard encouragement used by fitness instructors to pump up a class whose energy is starting to drag.

Digging deep, I told myself, "You're strong, Mary!"

Then I picked up my pace and finished the workout. I needed to see myself as strong, rather than as weak. I needed to claim my strength!

Throughout my life, my lanky build has often caused me to see myself as a weakling. And I've tended to believe that, because my natural preference was for exercising in short bursts, stamina and endurance were not my strong suits.

But staying fit—which today means three days of strength training every week and cardio the other days—has also taught me the truth about my strength, something a lot of women simply don't own. One of the ways I came to own my strength was by checking off one of the items on my bucket list at the age of 40, when I completed a marathon.

By challenging myself physically over the years, I've gained so much more than just a stronger body from my efforts. I've gained confidence and stamina. I've enhanced my sense of well-being. After finishing the marathon, with the help of my amazing running group, I knew that if I could accomplish that, I could do anything I put my mind to.

Rather than defeating myself with my own limiting beliefs, I now encourage myself with a new mantra: "Mary, you are strong!"

What about you?

- In what areas of your life have you not yet claimed your strength? Under what circumstances would you benefit from telling yourself, "You are strong!"

- Watch for places in your life where you reinforce your limitations with negative self-talk. Instead of journaling about the negative self-talk, instead start to compile a list of positive mantras that counteract any of your typical self-talk.

- Where are you teaching others to limit themselves in the messages you speak to them?

I'm free, I'm free

Stare Fear in the Face

"Love is what we were born with.
Fear is what we learned here."
— *Marianne Williamson*

My very first patient was a prisoner from the Ohio Penitentiary, shackled to the bed with handcuffs and accompanied 24/7 by a guard.

I had grown up pretty sheltered, attending Catholic school. My only exposure to crime had been on TV. So I was shaking when I went in to care for this middle-aged man in his prison uniform. But he surprised me. Maybe he could tell how scared I was, but he was patient with me. He thanked me. The scariest part of the situation turned out to be my own thinking.

What is the scariest thing you can think of? A plane crash? Terrorism? Public speaking?

Fear is a normal human response when we are faced with true danger. But much of the fear we experience is irrational and unnecessary. It's best described by the acronym FEAR: False Evidence Appearing Real.

Fear is healthy when it prompts us to protect ourselves and others from genuine danger. Healthy fear leads us to wear our seatbelts and prevents us from driving 80 miles an hour during an ice storm. But fear becomes unhealthy when we refuse to act on our dreams because we fear the risks involved.

If we stay in a career we hate because we fear the idea of trying a new field or going back to school, our fear sets us up for disappointment and dissatisfaction.

If we refuse to form close relationships with others because we fear they will hurt us, this fear sets us up for a lifetime of loneliness or isolation.

If fear prevents us from changing careers, trying new hobbies, or traveling to places that tug at our hearts, we will remain trapped by our insecurity and miss out on incredible experiences.

Although fears may try to harass you from time to time, Amelia Earhart correctly observed, "Fears are paper tigers. You can do anything you decide to do."

Remember the scene in "The Wizard of Oz" when the Scarecrow freaked out because the Tin Man told him the forest was filled with "lions and tigers and bears"? That was bad enough, but then Dorothy, the Tin Man, and the Scarecrow made "lions and tigers and bears, oh my!" their mantra for the rest of the scene! Soon they ran into the Cowardly Lion, who turned out not to be scary at all. Suppose they had turned back because they were afraid of something that just wasn't real?

To live our best lives, we must do what our best selves call us to do—even if we must "do it afraid." As Mark Twain pointed out, "Courage is resistance to fear, mastery of fear, not absence of fear."

Fear is just a feeling. We can't allow it to debilitate us and keep us from doing the great things for which we are destined.

The next time fear stalks you, stare right into its ugly face and declare, "Fear, you have no authority over my destiny! I choose to move forward in audacious faith."

What about you?

- Journal about how you normally handle the fears you encounter. Do you deal with them head-on? Deny they exist? Run from them? Cower in a corner and hope they go away?

- If fear is truly "**F**alse **E**vidence **A**ppearing **R**eal," what is some of the "false evidence" you've believed in the past?

- Journal about a time when you faced your fear and learned that it no longer held any power over you.

The old has
blown away

Nurture Your Health, Inside and Out

"All serious daring starts from within."
– Eudora Welty

The first rule for maximizing your total health is to nurture yourself from the inside out. The roots of many physical, social, and emotional problems are found in the deep places of the heart.

As a wellness nurse, I witnessed this unmistakable relationship between inner and outer health on a daily basis. Even though I often attempted to help people with issues such as obesity, diabetes, insomnia and high blood pressure, it became increasingly clear that these problems weren't exclusively physical in nature.

For example, those struggling with obesity often must address the spiritual and emotional turmoil that prompts them to overeat. Several of my patients were able to significantly lower their blood pressure by taking time to attend meditation classes where they could quiet their hearts and focus their minds on their spiritual life.

Likewise, researcher Kenneth Pelletier conducted a surprising five-year investigation of the health benefits that come from a life of altruism and the caring influence of family and friends. Amazingly, the absence of close, loving relationships posed a risk of disease just as significant as traditional risk factors such as adverse genetics, poor nutrition, or a lack of exercise.

Even the World Health Organization has recognized these relationships between our inner, outer and social health. Noting that good health is not merely the absence of disease or infirmity, the organization defines it as "a state of complete physical, mental, and social well-being." Not a bad definition!

Renowned neuroscientist Candace Pert adds, "Every thought, every feeling, every emotion we experience impacts us and is recorded in cellular memory." Yes, our entire physical, emotional, and spiritual makeup is connected and interrelated.

This means we must be good stewards not just of our physical well-being, but also of our mental, emotional, social, and spiritual personhood. Although people may act as if all these parts act independently, they're actually vitally connected. Each area is critically important and must be properly nurtured. If one area is neglected, it will have an adverse effect on the others.

How do you maintain your ***spiritual health***? For me, disciplines that play an important role in maintaining my spiritual health include prayer, meditation, study of sacred texts, and worship within a community of faith.

How can you enhance your ***mental and emotional health***? I do this by journaling, talking with close friends, reading novels, and doing fun things like seeing movies (cinema therapy!), going to concerts, shopping, or getting my hair and nails done. I also find it therapeutic to play my guitar and write songs. Maybe you enjoy gardening, cooking, taking a bubble bath, playing video games, or engaging in some hobby that replenishes your emotional tank.

And what about maintaining *physical health*? My spiritual and mental conditions are greatly enhanced when I also take care of my body. Getting a good night's sleep, eating nutritious meals, reducing stress, and taking time for an exercise class or a brisk walk in the park are important ingredients in my overall well-being.

Health is not automatic in any of these areas. It's a choice—a matter of countless decisions we make every day. To enhance our overall wellness and keep fit spiritually, emotionally and physically, we all need *intentionality* and *self-discipline*.

What about you?

- Balance is an important part of a healthy life. Consider each of the following five areas, and determine on a scale of 1 to 10 (with 10 being the highest) how well you are doing in self-care:
    - Spiritual –
    - Mental –
    - Emotional –
    - Social –
    - Physical –

- Which is your lowest area of self-care? Develop an action plan to strengthen this area of your life.

- In your journal, explore how the mind-body-spirit connection has played out in your life. What connections can you see between your emotional or spiritual dis-ease and the way your body experiences physical dis-ease?

The new has
been released

Change Your Colors to Beat the Blues

"I have sometimes been wildly, despairingly, acutely miserable, racked with sorrow, but through it all, I still know that just to be alive is a grand thing."
– Agatha Christie

I'm not a doctor, a licensed counselor, or even a psych nurse, yet doctors frequently referred patients with symptoms of depression to my wellness program.

Some of these depressed patients clearly had needs beyond the scope of my expertise. They needed long-term counseling, psychotherapy, or medication—none of which were things I could provide. However, some of the simple tools of wellness often brought dramatic improvements in people's emotional health. I've seen people's depression lift when they took action to connect with their spiritual Source, to engage in healthy social interactions, and to change their diet and exercise patterns.

One such transformation took place in the life of a middle-aged woman who participated in my cancer support group; I'll call her Lynn. Although Lynn's cancer was in remission, she had been seriously depressed ever since her battle with the disease began. She was a graphic example of someone who was now healthy in body, but whose emotional health was still in jeopardy.

Lynn could have withdrawn from society and curled up in a fetal position the rest of her life. She had been through a lot, and it must have been tempting to wallow in self-pity.

Yet Lynn didn't do that. She stepped out of her comfort zone and joined the support group, where she participated in an exercise program, accepted spiritual input, and made some good friends. Her cloud of depression lifted at least partly because she discovered some positive attitudes and activities to replace the blues.

Chronic, clinical depression is a serious psychiatric condition. But most of us experience situational depression at some times in our lives. When we do, there are many options for beating the blues.

The mindset we need to cultivate when we're experiencing depression related to specific circumstances in our lives is actually fairly simple: We can "change our colors" by changing our attitudes and actions. Instead of wishing and hoping our surroundings or circumstances will change, we can start with changing ourselves!

The truth about depression is this:

- Depression is a universal human experience that we'll **all** face at one time or another, and to one degree or another.
- Even though depression is a virtually inevitable experience, that doesn't mean we must **stay** in the valley of despair forever.

It's in the valleys that we come face to face with our true selves, and where we discover and test our true strength. But there's no need to camp out in the valleys indefinitely—we are merely to "pass through" to the other side. Depression is not an experience that should come to stay, but rather one that comes to pass! And once we've passed through this place of trial, we will be far more able to comfort others.

I don't claim it's always quick or easy, but you can overcome the blues. So pack your bags and get ready to leave the valley of depression behind. It's time for an internal makeover.

What about you?

- Think about a time in your life when you experienced "the blues." What factors triggered your depression? What helped you recover your peace and joy?

- If you have an opportunity to help a friend recover from depression, what will you recommend to them? When do you think it's necessary to seek professional help?

I'm free, I'm free, free!

Stretch Out Your Withered Hand

*"We must not, in trying to think about how
we can make a big difference, ignore the small
daily differences we can make which, over time,
add up to big differences that we often cannot foresee."*
— Marian Wright Edelman

During a particularly low period of my life, even the basic activities of daily living were difficult. I found myself just trying to get through each day, plodding along as if in a daze.

Feeling totally burnt out, I continued my part-time job at the hospital, but with low energy and little motivation. Toward the end of my shift one day, I heard a baby crying and went to investigate. To my surprise, I discovered that the baby's mother had stepped out of the room, and the baby had ended up with his feet sticking out of the crib. I lowered the rail, picked up the redheaded three-month-old, and he immediately quit crying.

I will never forget what happened in that magic moment. Amazingly, as the baby was comforted in my arms, I found myself also comforted. I forgot my own pain as I reached out to comfort another.

For years I had heard people say that we are often healed as we reach out to heal others—that our needs are met not by focusing our attention on ourselves, but by seeking to meet the needs around us. But until that moment of compassion for a needy infant in the hospital, I had never experienced this amazing principle for myself.

Are you familiar with the story of Jesus healing a man's withered hand by commanding him to stretch it out? The man obediently complied, and in doing so his hand was perfectly restored!

What if we stretch out our withered hands, leaving behind our debilitating self-centeredness and turning love into action? Instead of nursing our hurt and focusing inward, what if we used our energy to help others by making meals for new moms or people who are disabled? What about buying a box of 20 thank-you cards and writing a special note to someone once a week?

My dad recently told me a touching story about this principle. In the 1940s, World War II was still raging and Americans faced rationing for the sake of the war effort. Many soldiers who had lost limbs defending the cause of freedom now roamed the country, homeless and emotionally lost. To see them in such a deplorable condition was gut-wrenching.

Grandma Blubaugh had six kids, a meager income, and not a lot of material possessions. But when these wandering veterans stopped at her tiny house, she would offer them whatever food she had available. Sometimes this was a hot plate or bowl from her dinner, but more often it was just a peanut butter and jelly sandwich. She would talk with these wounded men and hear their stories as they sat on her back steps and ate.

And in the process of helping these needy souls, I'm sure Grandma found some additional peace and solace for her own soul.

So whenever you struggle with grief or disappointment or depression, there's hope for healing in the simple act of reaching out with a withered hand.

What about you?

- Can you remember a specific time in your life when you reached out to help or encourage someone else? What did your actions do for your spirits?

- Write down one or two simple actions you can take every day to be a blessing to others.

Taking me beyond
myself, again and
again

Stilling Your Hunger

"Do not spoil what you have
by desiring what you have not."
– Ann Brashares

Being content has always been a challenge for me. I'm a go-getter who wants to experience everything life has to offer. I have "great expectations," and am easily disappointed when reality doesn't live up to my ideal. Although I have had some of the most fabulous opportunities anyone could hope to have, I am always hungering for more!

Having an insatiable hunger for life is good, for it can stir us to action and motivate us toward significant accomplishments. Yet in my case, much of the hunger is really a lack of contentment.

What do you hunger for today? Success? Recognition? Popularity? Intimacy? Financial security? Adventure? Purpose? At various times in my life I have hungered for each of these things, and more.

To my surprise, I've learned that my restless appetite won't be satisfied even if I do obtain all the earthly things I crave. Despite any material belongings or personal accomplishments, I still end up thirsting for more. The reason, I've come to believe, is that none of those things can substitute for what we really crave. Nearly always, the things we think will fill us up are too superficial to satisfy our real hunger.

We all crave a sense of deep and lasting satisfaction. Beyond our material success and possessions, we want healthy relationships, a sense of purpose, and qualities such as vitality, resilience, and optimism.

Happiness isn't really as complicated as we often make it. Allan K. Chalmers gives us a pretty good summary when he says, "The grand essentials of happiness are: something to do, something to love, and something to hope for." Pretty simple, really.

And one of my favorite insights comes from Chinese philosopher Lao Tzu, who observed, "Contentment is the greatest treasure." In other words, the path to happiness can be found in wanting what we *already have*!

So let's try to still our hunger by embracing what is eternal and true. Let's put people above possessions, fertilizing the grass on our own side of the fence instead of coveting the grass on the other side that always seems to look so much greener.

What about you?

- What are some of the things you've typically craved in your life? Has your pursuit led you closer to your life purpose and your best self? Did satisfying those cravings lead to more cravings?

- What do you have today that you're grateful for? How might things change if you committed to expressing gratitude for something you already have, whenever you hunger for something you don't have?

- How often do you say you "need" something, when in actuality you merely "want" something? Journal about the difference between a need and a want. Commit to eliminating the word "need" from your vocabulary, except related to life's basic necessities: food, shelter, health, reliable (not luxurious) transportation, and clean clothes.

Taking me beyond myself to places I've never been

Safe People – and Those Who Aren't

"A relationship – it shouldn't be too small or too tight or even a little scratchy."
– Deb Caletti

I've been blessed with a few lifelong friends who have stuck with me through thick and thin. They are always ready to help if I have a need, and I can "let my hair down" and tell them anything, without fear of rejection. They have proven themselves trustworthy over the years, and they always bring out the best in me.

However, I've also had to dig deep into my heart to understand why I sometimes tolerate relationships with people who want to manipulate me or tear me down. In many cases, I've initially been attracted to such people because they seemed to be "experts"— with special insights or skills that seemingly could make my life better. But my openness to their expertise put me in a vulnerable position that eventually caused me to be hurt by the relationship.

Of course, sometimes we have no alternative but to be around someone who is "unsafe"—perhaps a relative, boss, or neighbor. There's no shame in concluding that some people aren't safe or healthy for us, but we should try to keep our contacts with such people to a minimum. When we must, we are wise to put on our "invisible force shield" to deflect the toxicity of these people. I have one friend who envisions herself surrounded by impenetrable light, which keeps her feeling safe and protected.

Even the healthiest of relationships can go through times of friction and be tested and refined in the fires of life. The key is in being able to spot the relationships that are worth refining in the fires and which ones we need to release.

Here's the best gauge I can offer: Tried and true friends seek to encourage you and help you become the best you can be.

What about you?

- List the 10 people who have had the greatest impact on your life, either positively or negatively. Categorize these people in one of three columns: positive, toxic, or mixed.

- As you review this list, do you see repetitive patterns in each column? Can you identify characteristics that mark the healthy relationships? What qualities of those relationships have enriched your life? What qualities in the toxic relationships have been detrimental to your life? What initially attracted you to the people who show up in your dysfunctional relationships?

Like a child that is
weaned

Posted: No Trespassing

"Don't compromise yourself. You are all you've got."
– Janis Joplin

I once dreamed I was a human pincushion.

In my dream, I sat passively in a basement, allowing family, friends, and co-workers to stick pins in me. I was so compliant that I even joined them in sticking the pins into my body.

After allowing this for quite some time, I suddenly was gripped with a fierce anger and morphed into the Incredible Hulk. The pins shot out from my body like bullets, and everyone ran for cover.

When I woke up, I realized that this dream provided some vital insights into my need for boundaries. I saw that I had often allowed people to stick pins in me, and that the fault was more mine than theirs. Even though I eventually rose up in anger and demanded that people quit causing me pain, I was unwise to wait until my anger reached the boiling point. I needed healthy boundaries that would keep me from getting to that point of desperation.

Many women struggle with this issue, because we were taught to be unselfish and turn the other cheek. This becomes unbalanced when we allow that idea to be recast as polite acquiescence as people walk all over us, bully us or even abuse us.

Because of her mental illness, my Mom sometimes treated me like that human pincushion in my dream. I had to learn, as an adult, to handle it differently than I had been able to handle it as a kid. I remember a day I was staying with Mom while Dad ran an errand. Her anger and panic got the better of her, and she began lashing out at me verbally. I knew what I had to do: I said, "Mom, I love you, but I don't have to stand here and listen to you talk to me like that."

Then I left the house, closed myself up in the garage, sat in my car and waited for my Dad to return. It was the first time I had stood up to her and Mom didn't like it one bit. But for me, it was a turning point.

We all need to set boundaries and we must maintain them. From time to time, we may need to tell certain people that they are infringing on our personhood. We're all entitled to establish the limits that define who we are and who we are not—boundaries that assert our rights and distinguish our identity from the identities of those around us.

We have a right to occupy space on the planet, just as they do.

Yes, we want to be approachable, but we also need to know when to put out a sign that says, "No trespassing. You have gone far enough. Back off!"

What about you?

- Do you have a clear sense of what healthy boundaries look like in your life? What boundaries have you set with family members, friends, neighbors, and coworkers?

- How do you react to the idea of determining your personal boundaries and then protecting them?

- Journal about a time in your life when someone violated your boundaries. How could you have handled the situation differently?

- Does anyone in your life consistently violate your boundaries? Ask yourself how clearly you've communicated your boundaries to this person. How can you start today to renegotiate the relationship and set boundaries that are right for you?

I have stilled
my weary soul
within me

Falling Off
the Edge
of the Plate

*"By and large, mothers and housewives
are the only workers who do not have regular time off.
They are the great vacationless class."*
– Anne Morrow Lindbergh

I n my teens and twenties, I tried to imitate the Energizer Bunny. Constantly on the move, I pushed the limits of my endurance and dared my spiritual, emotional, and physical batteries to run out of energy. And often they did!

Because I had a hard time saying "no" to people, I regularly took on far more than I could handle. I continually added more to my plate, while never removing anything. At times I nearly fell off the edge of that plate!

After I had babies, I tried to maintain all the activities I had done before. And even as my body got older, I still tried to display the vitality I had as a teenager. Over time, the situation escalated as the kids grew up and became more active themselves—dance, piano, violin, sports, Bible study. With life's treadmill going faster and faster, I had no idea how to get off and take a rest.

Have you ever felt like this? Have you bitten off more than you could chew, only to find yourself choking on it?

I have discovered that many problems in my life have been the direct result of losing my "margins." In his excellent book, *Margin*, Dr. Richard Swenson defines a margin as the space between us and our limits, the gap between rest and exhaustion. He points out that our society has frantically gobbled up the margins that once protected our spiritual, emotional, physical, and financial well-being.

Many of us have gotten so used to living without margins that we assume it's the only option. "Living life on the edge" is viewed as an admirable trait. Meanwhile, we are failing in our relationships, our finances, and our health—maxed out in every area of our lives and without a clue how to get revitalized. Women are especially guilty of this as we struggle to please everybody, take care of everybody, and fill all the roles society expects us to fill.

We have been created with a need for clear limits and boundary lines. But how can we get these margins back if they seem to have disappeared?

One of the keys is to reestablish our spiritual and physical disciplines. Daily prayer or meditation, a weekly day of rest, regular exercise, healthy eating, adequate sleep, and periodic vacations are all practical aids to keep us from running out of steam.

But our margins will never be restored without a firm commitment on our part to go against the tide of our busy society. It will take determination to learn the art of contentment, rest, scaling back, and actively pursuing a new simplicity in every area of life, including relationships, finances, time, and health.

What about you?

- We need margins in every area of our lives, including our relationships, our finances, our time, and our health. Journal about some areas of your life where you struggle the most to maintain proper margins.

- Where in your life can you eliminate clutter and emotional overload in order to regain margins?

- What are you willing to give up in order to regain your margins?

There is a hidden
door, seems like
a secret

Naysayers and Other Donkeys

"The question isn't who's going to let me;
it's who is going to stop me."

– Ayn Rand

When I graduated from high school, my parents threw me a big graduation party and invited lots of friends and relatives. It was a wonderful celebration, a time to look forward to a bright and happy future. I had received a partial scholarship to a nearby college, and was very excited about the next step on my journey in life.

But not everyone was so excited about my prospects. One of my relatives from out of town asked me what I was planning to do. I replied that I was going to college to be a nurse. He paused for a second, and then looked me right in the eyes, saying: "You'll never make it!"

I was shocked. His words kept reverberating in my head: "You'll never make it!" I couldn't believe that someone who should have been encouraging my success and well-being was now betting against me.

Finally, I regained my composure and told him he was wrong. "Yes, I will make it," I told him firmly. And at that moment I decided that no matter what challenges I faced in nursing school, I was going to prove my naysaying relative wrong!

What if aviator Amelia Earhart had listened to her naysayers? Steve Jobs and the Wright brothers had their share of naysayers. And few people who have watched Susan Boyle's first performance on "Britain's Got Talent" can forget the expressions of doubt on the faces of the judges and audience members when the 47-year-old unknown singer announced she would sing "I Dreamed a Dream." But she certainly silenced their naysaying, didn't she?

I bet you've had some naysayers in your life, too. We all have. The question is whether we listen to them or ignore them.

I'll admit, even though I was determined to succeed in nursing school and prove my naysaying relative wrong, it wasn't easy. Halfway through my first semester I got mononucleosis and had to be sent home to rest and recover. Was I tempted to quit? Absolutely. Instead I persevered.

Good grades didn't come easy for me in nursing school, and many other times I was ready to give up. But each time I was tempted to quit, I remembered the words of my pessimistic relative. Before long, I was graduating from nursing school and starting my job at the prestigious Columbus Children's Hospital.

Remember this classic quote from President Theodore Roosevelt—a man who faced plenty of naysayers along the way:

It is not the critic who counts; not the man who points out how the strong man stumbles, or where the doer of deeds could have done them better. The credit belongs to the man who is actually in the arena, whose face is marred by dust and sweat and blood, who strives valiantly, who errs and comes short again and again; because there is no effort without error and shortcoming; but who does actually strive to do the deeds; who knows the great enthusiasms, the great devotions; who spends himself for a worthy cause; who at the best knows, in the end, the triumph of high achievement; and who, at the worst, if he fails, at least he fails while daring greatly, so that his place shall never be with those cold and timid souls who know neither victory nor defeat.

Naysayers will inevitably try to throw cold water on worthy projects. They are unhappy people. They are fear-based people. But they can fill a very powerful role in our lives as the incentive for tenaciously pursuing success. I didn't achieve my goals merely in spite of my naysayer. I used his pessimism as a catalyst for my success!

What about you?

- Journal about some of the naysayers in your life, paying particular attention to how they served as an incentive to succeed. Write to a few of them, in your journal, and express either your forgiveness or your gratitude for their attitude toward your dreams.

- Examine yourself to see where you may be filling the role of naysayer in someone's life. What can you do to change your role?

Concealed from
my vision

Who's Pressing Your Buttons?

"Parents know how to push your buttons because,
hey, they sewed them on."
– Camryn Manheim

In my work as a nurse, I've spent a lot of time around grumpy, angry, demanding and unpleasant people. Being sick, or having a loved one who is sick, brings out the worst in a lot of us.

As a nurse, the last thing I need if I am going to remain sane and have a positive impact on these people is to allow their "worst" to press my buttons, which inevitably brings out my worst. And as a sensitive, artistic person, I definitely have my share of buttons.

Each of us has hypersensitive areas in our personality—"buttons" that are painful when pressed. Some of the buttons are clearly apparent, just begging the mischievous people around us to push them. Other buttons lurk in hidden minefields just beneath the surface, ready to explode if some unsuspecting person accidentally infringes on their territory.

Some buttons are common to humankind, such as guilt, shame, inferiority, rejection, or control. But we all have our own areas of particular hypersensitivity, based upon painful past experiences. For example, someone whose parents got divorced might be particularly sensitive to issues of separation and rejection. And a person who lost a loved one recently might still have some sore spots connected with abandonment or the grieving process.

Unless you become a hermit, someone is bound to press your buttons from time to time. It may be your spouse, your boss, a co-worker, one of your kids, or someone in your church or neighborhood, even the friend of a friend on Facebook. But sooner or later, your buttons will be pushed.

Although having our buttons pushed is inevitable, reacting like a hidden landmine is not inevitable. We always have a choice about how we react to the pushing of our buttons. It's okay to express hurt, and it's important to set boundaries. But it is critical to express ourselves in an appropriate manner.

The good thing about having our buttons pushed is that we can no longer ignore the sensitive areas where we need to heal. Our buttons mark the spot.

What about you?

- Review your life and see if you can remember specific times when people pressed your buttons and you reacted poorly. What patterns do you see? What buttons are most sensitive in your life?

- Are you aware of the buttons of your loved ones? Can you actively demonstrate your love in the way you navigate those sensitive areas for your loved ones?

- Where do your buttons create friction with your loved ones' buttons?

Camouflaged
by my circumstance

Listen, for Heaven's Sake

"Part of doing something is listening.
We are listening. To the sun. To the stars. To the wind."
– Madeleine L'Engle

I've found that many of the conflicts in my life are the result of not listening. Too often I jump to conclusions in my relationships with people, assuming that I know what they are thinking, even though I haven't really listened to what they've said.

As the old adage goes, "There's a reason God gave us two ears and only one mouth." But this is difficult for most of us.

As a nurse, this was an important lesson for me. I had to grow in my ability to listen to the doctors, coworkers, and managers, as well as to my patients and their families. I had to learn to ask "clarifying questions." In the hospital setting, listening is not just a nice option—people's lives are at stake! Becoming a good listener has helped bring clarity and comfort to stressful and dangerous situations, and has helped ward off much potential conflict.

Listening is an art to be learned, not something that comes naturally. Effective listening involves warmth, empathy, and respect. It means looking people in the eyes and letting them know we have really heard what they've said. It takes discipline and selflessness to be attentive, interested, and concerned.

My daughter recently read Dale Carnegie's classic book, *How to Win Friends and Influence People*. Although the book contains loads of helpful principles, it all boils down to this: *Most people love to talk about **themselves***. Naturally, most of us have the same tendency to love talking about ourselves. In a more recent book on the subject, *The Charisma Myth*, author Olivia Fox Cabane writes, "Listening lays the groundwork for the presence that is fundamental to charisma."

So being a good conversationalist—as well as winning friends and influencing people—actually starts with being a good listener when people tell us their story or share their concerns.

What about you?

- On a scale of 1 to 10 (with 10 being the highest), rate your present skills as a listener.

- Ask someone close to you for feedback on whether they feel you truly listen to them—and ask if they have any suggestions for improvement.

- Practice listening. Practice being the one who listens and not the one who speaks. Evaluate how your social interactions change as you listen more, speak less.

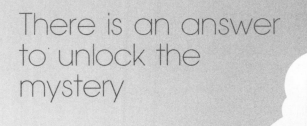

There is an answer
to unlock the
mystery

Be a Thermostat, Not a Thermometer

*"I have the choice of being constantly
active and happy or introspectively passive and sad.
Or I can go mad by ricocheting in between."*
– Sylvia Plath

Everyone on the Pediatrics floor was walking on eggshells around this particular father. His young daughter's heart was failing, her body shutting down. He was reacting by behaving like a control freak, micromanaging everything, threatening to change doctors when he didn't like what was happening.

So when we went into her room to care for her, most of us had to force ourselves to focus on caring for the little girl instead of trying not to anger the father.

Finally, I did what no one else wanted to do: I sat with him and said, "I can't fix this situation, but is there anything you want me to do?"

He started to cry.

The one thing I can't do as a nurse is let the mood of patients and their families determine my mood. Yet it's something so many of us do, especially in our personal lives. So I try to remember that there is a big difference between a thermostat and a thermometer. A thermostat sets the temperature. A thermometer only reflects the temperature.

Too often, I find myself acting like a thermometer, with my mood bouncing up and down based on the people and events around me.

By nature I am a sensitive and intuitive person. This sensitivity has its advantages, for I am often able to pick up on the "vibes" of others, sensing whether they are happy, angry or sad. However, my sensitivity also causes some problems. Sometimes I literally need to turn it off in order to live in peace with other people.

As a child I often felt responsible for the moods and emotions of those around me; this is common in a household where mental illness is present. It started in my family, then extended to my other relationships as well.

It was many years before I saw how unhealthy this mindset is. It wasn't easy to discover that I could not control the moods of others, nor should I allow their moods to affect mine.

What a great joy it is to finally realize that we need not allow other people to impose their moods or miseries on us. We are responsible for our own attitudes and actions, and no one should be permitted to make us feel mad, sad, or bad. There will be days when our boss, family, or friends will be disgruntled, but that should not determine our state of mind.

A joy-filled person can transform the atmosphere of his or her environment, because joy is not based on emotions or on circumstances. It is a consciously chosen mindset, designed to spread light in darkness.

We may not be able to immediately change our circumstances, but we can—and must—change our attitude and how we respond. As author and leadership coach Zig Ziglar says, "Your attitude, not your aptitude, will determine your altitude." It's up to us!

So how can you be a thermostat today? Smile at people. Greet them with kind words. Praise others around you. Speak respectfully to your coworkers, even if they seem to behave like jerks. Strive for excellence. Dress well. Exert your fullest effort at what you do best. And honor others for their differences.

Who knows? You might just change the world.

What about you?

- Take an informal survey of your five closest friends or loved ones; ask if they see you as a thermostat (bringing about positive changes to the situations you face) or a thermometer (merely reflecting the external events in your life). Openly welcome their opinions, and once they've given them, thank them and encourage them to tell you more.

- Journal about a situation you can help to change, listing specific attitudes and actions that will make the change possible.

A key to open
obscurity, my eyes
couldn't see

Clear Your Log-Jammed Eyes

"Cut others some slack!"
– Gretchen Rubin

I've been told that my blue-green eyes are pretty—but you should see them when they get "log-jammed"!

Maybe you've never heard of this condition. It's described in the Bible in Matthew 7:3: "Why do you look at the speck of sawdust in your brother's eye and pay no attention to the plank in your own eye?"

Like cataracts that form on the lenses of our eyes and cloud our vision, planks in our eyes have numerous ill effects.

First, if we are consumed with analyzing the speck of sawdust in someone else's eye, we have set ourselves up as judges, which is always a bad idea.

Second, having a judgmental attitude makes it hard to get along with people. After years of being a rather prickly person because of my critical attitude toward others, I have discovered an amazing truth: People tend to like me if they think I like them! In contrast, people with log-jammed eyes insist on judging everyone they meet; few people make the cut and graduate into the role of friend.

Third, when our eyes are log-jammed, we are blind to the issues we need to deal with in our own lives. The ironic thing about log-jam syndrome is that when we see a fault in others, it is usually one of the same faults we have!

In other words…if you spot it, you've got it!

Ouch.

No one is perfect. But when our eyes are log-jammed, we have no mercy for the shortcomings of others. We are showing them no love when we point the finger of judgment at them.

So what is the remedy for this terrible condition? Compassion. If we want to receive mercy, we must extend mercy to others.

The best way to prepare ourselves for compassion is to seek to understand *why* a person is behaving a certain way. In the introduction to his book *The 7 Habits of Highly Effective People*, Stephen R. Covey shares a profound experience he had on a subway ride. He noticed a father with two rambunctious little boys who were hyper and disruptive. When the father was asked (rather critically) why he was allowing this to go on, he replied, "We just got back from the hospital, where their mother died. I don't know how to handle it, and I guess they don't either."

Covey concludes, as St. Francis did in his famous prayer, we should "seek first to understand, and then to be understood."

A friend who is a spiritual coach tells me that whenever she must spend time with people who push her buttons, she prepares herself by praying to see the people who trouble her the way God sees them. She says it transforms her interactions with those people. "And it's one prayer that is always answered, and answered immediately."

If all else fails, some rose-colored glasses may be necessary to fix your log-jammed eyes. They'll filter out the negative traits of others and highlight their positive traits.

What about you?

- Who are the three people in your life that you spend the most time with? When you think of them, do their positive or their negative attributes come to mind first? If you're more aware of their negative characteristics, make a concerted effort to focus on the good qualities of others.

- Spend some time reflecting on and journaling about any "blind spots" in your life that are hindering your relationships with others.

I found the way,
I don't have
to stay

Get Out
of Jail—FREE!

*"Not forgiving is like drinking rat poison
and then waiting for the rat to die."*
– Anne Lamott

When someone hurts me, my immediate impulse is sometimes to lash out in anger. I want the person who hurt me to feel what I am feeling. That's a pretty common human response.

A better response—and the only response that is guaranteed to cut short my own time in the prison of resentment and anger —is to *forgive*.

When we hold on to offenses we think others have committed, we are the ones who end up in a self-imposed hell, sentenced to carrying around our bitterness wherever we go. I know from first-hand experience that harboring unforgiveness hurts us more than it hurts the person we haven't forgiven. Refusing to forgive keeps us locked up with the very person we hate. And there is only one door out of this prison: We need to wholeheartedly forgive. Forgiveness is the key to escape from bondage.

I've had plenty of opportunities to learn the fine art of forgiveness. Sometimes I've passed the test; other times, this hasn't been easy for me. I have made lots of excuses to justify my failure to forgive someone I think has wronged me. One of my arguments has been that I simply don't feel forgiveness—but I must forgive anyway. Forgiveness is not a feeling; it is a decision.

I've also thought I could wait until the other person had a change of heart and apologized to me. But that could mean waiting a long time! Meanwhile, the pain of the situation simmers in my heart until I become bitter.

Forgiveness begins with removing myself as the judge, and recognizing that I have a capacity to do the very same thing as the one who offended me. Sometimes I even get to the point where I can actually thank those who have offended me. For as physician and author Gerald Jampolsky observes, "When I am able to resist the temptation to judge others, I can see them as teachers of forgiveness in my life, reminding me that I can only have peace of mind when I forgive rather than judge."

In their book *From Age-ing to Sage-ing*, authors Zalman Schacter-Shalomi and Ronald Miller provide this great analogy about forgiveness:

When I refuse to forgive someone who has wronged me, I mobilize my own inner criminal justice system to punish the offender. As judge and jury, I sentence the person to a long prison term without pardon and incarcerate him in a prison that I construct from bricks and mortar of a hardened heart. Now as jailor and warden, I must spend as much time in prison as the prisoner I am guarding. All the energy that I put into maintaining the prison system comes out of my energy budget. From this point of view, bearing a grudge is very costly, because long-held feelings of anger, resentment, and fear drain my energy and imprison my vitality and creativity.

So if you're still locked in a jail cell of unforgiveness—a cell of your own creation—it's time to break out!

What about you?

- Journal about some of the time you've spent in a prison of your own making because of a refusal to forgive.

- Make a list of people you've harmed who have forgiven you. Journal about how it feels to be on the receiving end of forgiveness.

- Make a list of anyone who has wronged you, and make a decision to forgive them and release them from the offense. Don't stop until you experience deep peace and relief in your heart.

The open door I've
been lookin' for

Does Anger Rule You or Fuel You?

"If you stay in the company of anger, pain, or hurt, happiness will find someone else to visit."

– Kristen Crockett

Psychologists have pointed out that depression is often the result of anger turned inward. Maybe that's why depression's grip on my life was broken when I turned my anger into righteous indignation.

In today's violent world, it's easy to get the impression that anger is always a bad thing. Yet that's not true. Anger is just a feeling and it can be okay to be angry at times, as long as we don't allow anger to provoke us to make destructive choices. And we must avoid holding on to our anger, which can make us miserable, prickly people.

After years of cyclical bouts with depression, I recognized anger boiling within me—not toward people but toward the darkness that had held me captive to depression. This fury welled up with righteous indignation against the lies that had brought me to such hopelessness. The first stronghold demolished was the lie that continuing in sadness was "the way it would always be" for me. I began to see myself as destined for joy instead of defeated by depression.

You see, anger can be a healthy thing if it prompts us to positive change.

"Anger is OK," my friend Kathrine Lee observes. "But let it FUEL you toward change, not RULE you into bitterness."

Healthy anger has enabled me to solve daunting problems and overcome long-standing fears and obstacles. It has helped me express my personal values with courage and conviction, moving forward toward the kind of life I desire. When my strength was at low ebb, healthy anger sparked focus and energy.

Anger happens, but make it productive.

What about you?

- Journal about how you've experienced anger in your life. What patterns can you see in the kinds of situations that trigger your anger? What opportunities for positive change do you see in those patterns? Can you find times when anger could have been converted into fuel for positive action?

- How do you typically handle anger? How do you express it?

I'm walkin'
through, on a
path that's new

Receive and Share 'The Blessing'

"When you wish someone joy, you wish them peace, love, prosperity, happiness... all the good things."
– Maya Angelou

My walk home from school as a little girl took me past my grandparents' house. Many days, I stopped to have cookies with Grandpa Blubaugh, who would say, "Mary Frances, tell me how your day was." After we had cookies and a heart-to-heart talk, we would often play cards. Or he would ask me to sing for him.

I still love cookies with vanilla filling in the middle, just like the ones I shared with Grandpa Blubaugh.

When I was in college, Grandpa had a stroke. Whenever I visited, first in the hospital and later in the Catholic nursing home where he went for recovery, I would take my guitar and play and sing for Grandpa. He was unable to speak because of the stroke, but one day I stopped playing before he was ready and Grandpa made a great effort to take my hand and put it back on the guitar so I would continue.

That day, Grandpa gave me his blessing on my music, propelling me on to later success as a singer and songwriter.

I also received a blessing in a remarkable way at my wedding. As my dad and I stood arm-in-arm before he walked me down the aisle, he looked me in the eyes and said, "Mary, I'm proud of you!"

That may not sound like much of a blessing, unless you know what came before it. My family was Catholic, made up of many priests and nuns. When I went to college, I left the Catholic faith and was re-baptized as a Protestant. My Dad was so hurt by my decision that he told me I was no longer welcome in their home.

So his giving of the blessing on my wedding day represented a powerful reconciliation for us. We both had to fight back tears as the wedding march began and we proceeded down the aisle.

One of the most profound lessons of life is that we all tend to treat others in exactly the same way as we perceive that God treats us. If we experience grace and kindness, we will inevitably be gracious and kind to others. But if we see our God as a harsh taskmaster, we will impart that same judgmental spirit on to the people surrounding us.

I can tell you with confidence that God wants to bless you and make you a blessing to others.

According to authors Gary Smalley and John Trent, "The Blessing" can be defined as "The knowledge that someone in the world loves us and accepts us unconditionally." Many people go their entire lives without receiving the blessing.

My heart was touched a few years ago when a pastor told of praying for a 50-year-old man who was a leader in his country. The pastor felt called to tell the man that in God's eyes he was "a fine boy." Surprisingly, the man broke down and began to weep as he heard these simple words. His whole life, he had hoped in vain to hear words of affirmation from his own father.

You see, no matter how young or old we are, the approval of our parents affects how we view ourselves and whether we are able to successfully love and accept others. Fortunately, God intervenes at times to give us the blessing, even if we haven't received it from the people in our lives.

For many of us, our lives are a quest for the blessing. Sometimes, the main thing blocking us from experiencing love and favor is our belief that the blessing comes in only one package, from only one source.

Sometimes, we mistakenly think we can only give the blessing if we have received it from a source that seems to withhold it. The truth is, we can always give the blessing. When we do, we will receive it as well. How that works is one of the mysteries of the universe; but I know it to be true.

What about you?

- Journal about the times in your life when others encouraged you and gave you the blessing.

- Look around you and ask for the clarity to understand who hungers for the blessing from you. How can you become a giver of the blessing?

And now
I'm free!

Celebrate the Seasons of Friendship

*"Friendship is the most important thing
— not career or housework, or one's fatigue —
and it needs to be tended and nurtured."*
– Julia Child

Perhaps you learned this lesson long ago, but it's something I must be reminded of from time to time: If we're going to fulfill our purpose and reach our destination, we need other people in our lives. As John Donne famously pointed out, "No man is an island entire of itself; every man is a piece of the continent, a part of the main." And more recently, one of our country's most powerful women reminded the world that "it takes a village."

None of us is self-sufficient. No one succeeds alone. We are part of humanity and must learn to get along and work together.

This means cultivating true friendships. But we also must realize that we only have a capacity for a limited number of genuine friendships at any one time in our life. (Alright, maybe you have hundreds or even thousands of friends on Facebook. That's not the kind of "friend" I'm talking about here, but it is true that our online communities can become one component of the powerful network we need on our spiritual and emotional journeys.)

Our relational support system will be comprised of different types of friends, each with its own special function and value. Some friends ***correct*** us…others ***direct*** us. Some make us ***think***… while others help us ***feel***. Some are catalysts for ***lofty dreams***… and others excel at bringing us back to ***reality*** when we're just deceiving ourselves. At one time or another, we need all of these in our entourage.

I've also found that friendships go through various seasons. Life changes. People switch jobs or move to other neighborhoods or cities. Couples who've been our friends sometimes get divorced. And it's hard to maintain all the friendships we had in high school or college or on a particular job.

If you haven't already experienced the seasons of friendship, I'm sure you will. Some friendships thrive when you're a newlywed…have young children…go back to work…become an empty-nester…or eventually retire. Sometimes life is simply taking us in a different direction from those we once walked with closely. Sometimes priorities change. Values change. Beliefs change. The things that once brought us together are no longer lining up, and perhaps they are even at odds.

Of course, a few close relationships can endure these changes in life's seasons, but some will diminish. This is sad and painful in some ways—but it's reality.

Let's be honest: When friends exit our lives, whether abruptly or gradually, it hurts. We have to adjust and reassess. We may even have to go through a grieving process over the lost relationship. But none of this should shock or surprise us. The fact is, people will come and go in our lives. This isn't necessarily anyone's fault. You may be tempted to feel guilty or ashamed...but you shouldn't.

But we do need to understand when to keep pursuing and nurturing a relationship, and when to let it go. When we come to a fork in the road regarding a friendship, we need to decide whether to continue the journey together—even if it's now long distance—or whether to pursue different paths.

Being separated from a true friend will leave a hole in your heart. Yet sometimes there's no other way for both of you to move on and grow as the people you need to be in a new season of your life.

What about you?

- Who was your first "best friend"? Who is your closest friend today? Journal about how those friendships differ.

- Journal about the common threads that you can see in all the deepest friendships of your life. What can you learn from your friendship history?

- On a scale of 1 to 10 (with 10 being the highest), how much value have you put on finding and cultivating quality friendships?

- Make a list of the true friends in your life today. Prioritize the value of these relationships in your current season of life.

There is a pathway
leading me out
of here

Discover Your Unique Voice

"With stammering lips and insufficient sounds
I strive and struggle to deliver
the right music of my nature."
– Elizabeth Barrett Browning

As a singer and songwriter, I have tried many different styles of music in the quest to find my own "personal sound." I originally found myself imitating the styles of others, hoping to find my own niche in the process. Seals and Crofts, John Denver, The Eagles, America, and Bread were some of the early influences on my taste in music. When I was recording the song "Hide Me in the Shadow" on my "Carry Me" CD, I felt as if I finally had "found my voice." We were in a recording studio in somebody's basement. I was recording the lead vocal and had a sense that the Celtic sound of this particular song fit my voice in a way nothing else did. Later, one of the women who came in to harmonize heard what I had already recorded and started to cry. She said, "Something came down from heaven."

Something special happened in that basement recording studio when I sang that song. I recognized that this is the kind of music I was born to sing!

It felt as though I had finally "come home" to my true self. In that magic moment, it was as if I had a taste of my destiny.

Each of us has been created uniquely, with our own special song to sing. When we "find our voice"—our authentic expression of something we love that makes us feel as if we've come home to our true self—others will enjoy it, too. "Hide Me in the Shadow" has been one of my most popular songs on radio stations across the country.

I love this quote from Olympic gold medalist Eric Liddell, whose story is chronicled in the movie "Chariots of Fire": "God made me fast. And when I run, I feel His pleasure."

What about you?

- Journal about your journey to discover your own voice. How long has it taken you to sing in that voice rather than just echoing other voices?

- Describe a time in your life when you felt truly alive and able to fully express your best self and the talents you've been blessed with.

I don't have to be
where I am, stuck
beneath, trapped
beneath

If the
Shoe Fits

"There is a fountain of youth: it is your mind,
your talents, the creativity you bring to your
life and the lives of the people you love.
When you learn to tap this source,
you will truly have defeated age."
– Sophia Loren

Several years ago, my husband and I had the opportunity to pastor a church. The previous pastor and his wife had served there since the church began, and they had been wonderful leaders. The pastor's wife was extremely gifted, and she had been involved in virtually every area of the church's ministry.

By contrast, I was still fairly young. I had never been involved in leadership before. In addition, I had two children still under the age of five, so my time and energy for church involvement felt very limited.

As the time approached for my husband to be installed as the new pastor, I began getting cold feet. Finally, I told a family friend about my certainty that I was completely incapable of filling the shoes of this remarkable pastor's wife.

My friend just smiled and said, "I think she's going to take her shoes with her!"

Of course! He was absolutely right, and I was so relieved!

Remember how much trouble Dorothy brought down on herself by taking over those ruby red slippers? Most of us, of course, believe we would keep on walking before slipping the shoes off a dead witch and slipping them on ourselves. Yet most of us have been guilty of doing something like that at times.

We don't need to fill anyone's shoes but our own. This simple principle brought me great freedom. I began to see that pastors' wives come in many different shapes, sizes, talents, temperaments and personality types. I didn't need to fit into someone else's shoes! I had shoes of my *own* to fill!

Kathrine Lee, the cofounder of The Source, calls this "living out your design." Whether you've discovered it or not, your Creator has designed a pair of shoes just for you—no need to take anybody else's ruby red slippers.

We all know what it's like to try on shoes. We take pair after pair out of their boxes and put them on our feet. Some pinch our toes, some rub our heels, some just don't feel right for reasons we can't quite figure out. But sooner or later we slip into a pair of shoes that feels as if it had been specially made for our feet. Sold!

Maybe you remember a time in your life when you tasted your destiny. It may have been for a season of time, or perhaps it was for only a moment, but it gave you a glimpse of what you were created for.

That's the fit we're all looking for. Don't give up until you find it!

What about you?

- Make a list of your five most distinctive gifts, abilities, and passions—your unique "shoes." If you get stumped, ask a few of your closest friends for input.

- Describe a magic moment in your life when you experienced a glimpse of the ruby red slippers that had been made just for you and the joy of fulfilling the design for your life. Contrast that with the pinched-toe feeling of trying to fill a role that wasn't right for you.

A passage
uncovered
suddenly, taking
me where I
need to be

Blinders
Help You See

"Ninety percent of my game is mental.
It's my concentration that has gotten me this far."
– Chris Evert

I always thought blinders on horses were cruel, but I'm having second thoughts.

As Americans, we live in a very distracting society. We have responsibilities that are often bewildering and draining: family, job, finances, health, church, and friends all compete for our time and attention. If we do not have our eyes fixed steadfastly on the goal line, there will always be people who have other agendas for our lives. Our best life will elude us unless we can learn how to go through life wearing blinders against the distractions.

Tennis phenomenon Venus Williams is known for her focus and determination. Throughout her career, this two-time Olympic gold medalist has encountered many hurdles and criticisms, but she's refused to let these distract her from tennis excellence.

In 2002 Venus attained her personal goal, which was to be ranked number one in the Women's Tennis Association. This was after winning at Wimbledon in 2000 and then defending her title there and at the U.S. Open. Since then, she has won the Wimbledon singles title five times. At the time this book was published, she had won 21 Grand Slam titles.

"I never thought anyone was better than me," Venus once commented in a New York Times interview. "Once you do that, you lose."

I want the focus and tenacity of Venus Williams. Instead of being worried or distracted by the obstacles in my way, I want to keep my eyes on the primary purpose for my life. Instead of zigging and zagging through life, I want to take the straightest line to the end zone. I don't want to let anything or anyone stop me in my mission.

When people ask us to participate in a certain activity, we have to ask ourselves: *Would this activity lead me in the direction of the goal line for my life?* As German writer and artist Johann Wolfgang von Goethe reminds us, "Things that matter most must never be at the mercy of things that matter least."

But this isn't easy to sort out unless we have a clear mission for our life. A personal mission statement provides us with a set of blinders, allowing us to block distractions and focus on actions that are in line with our calling and purpose in life.

What about you?

- Write your personal mission statement.
- List the priority actions that will support this personal mission statement.
- Set goals based on your priorities.
- Identify your top distractions. Be ruthless in identifying them and dealing with them when they show up in your life.

A way of escape
and now I'm free!

Survive and Thrive Through the Seasons of Life

"Continuity gives us roots; change gives us branches,
letting us stretch and grow and reach new heights."
– Pauline R. Kezer

Life was a whirlwind of continuous change and adjustment after high school. Living away from home for the first time and adapting to dorm life posed many challenges, and sometimes the nursing curriculum and financial obligations made me consider becoming a college dropout.

I got married halfway through my senior year of college. Although fun, that also brought me more adjustments and stress. Within months, I was graduating from nursing school and starting my new career as a pediatric nurse. Three years later, I was giving birth to my first child, Molly...followed within eight years by Abigail and Ben.

If life was a whirlwind when I was single or a newlywed, the pace only quickened when I was raising three children and chaperoning field trips and birthday parties, taxiing them to dance and music lessons, sports practice, and games. In the midst of this, we moved three times, from Ohio to Florida to North Carolina.

As the months and years whizzed by, all I could do was adopt the motto "Constant change is here to stay!"

Now that I have more free time I look forward to sharing my experiences and lessons to help and heal others.

I've discovered that each season of life has its own trials and joys, disillusionments and lessons, battles and victories. As my head spins to think of how fast these seasons have sped by, some old clichés come to mind. *Savor the moment. Take time to smell the roses.* Although these are great advice, they seem a little simplistic when life is moving a thousand miles an hour.

Each new season has a special purpose, a unique blessing. While winter seems to strip the trees of life, it's actually preparing them for greater fruitfulness in the coming springtime. What looks like death is laying the groundwork for a season of glorious rebirth.

Life is a journey. We were not designed to just stand still. And through every season of life, our Ultimate Source is with us, helping us not just to survive, but to thrive.

What about you?

- Describe the challenges and blessings of the season of life you are currently experiencing. Are you handling this season well? Are you living it fully?

- As you look ahead at the coming seasons of your life, how can you prepare to be your best in those seasons?

Letting go, moving
on, singing a
new song

Pace
the Race

"For me, slowing down has been a tremendous source of creativity…Creativity exists in the present moment. You can't find it anywhere else."
– Natalie Goldberg

When I was in middle school, I was the fastest girl around. I mostly ran sprints in those days.

I'm not as fast as I used to be, but that's okay; life isn't a sprint anyway. Success in life doesn't go to those who are the fastest, but to those who keep going for the long haul.

As I neared my 40th birthday, I got interested in running a marathon. I knew I would need some kind of instruction, so I signed up with the Jeff Galloway marathon program. I'm really glad I did. In training to run long races, it's very helpful to have others run with you and give you advice when you experience difficulties.

Jeff Galloway has a unique approach to running marathons. He advocates a strategy of running for five to eight minutes and then walking for one minute, until you've gone the entire 26.2 miles.

This strategy of taking regular breaks to walk and drink some water helps you pace yourself and avoid injuries that might cause you to quit the race. It also gives you a mini rest break every five minutes or so. Not surprisingly, those who take the mini rest breaks often end up outrunning those who don't.

During my six-month training period, there were many times on the long runs when I felt like giving up, something runners call "hitting the wall." However, with Jeff Galloway's program I was able to encourage myself with positive self-talk: *Mary, all you need to do is run another five minutes, and then you will have a walk break.*

This perspective was a huge help to me! I set an egg timer for five minutes and ran until it beeped. Then I set it for one minute and walked until it beeped again. Instead of facing the overwhelming prospect of running the entire 26.2-mile race, I just had to focus on running another five minutes until my next break. That didn't sound so hard! In fact, it was very doable.

I finished the full 26.2 miles of the Marine Corps Marathon in Washington, DC. And I accomplished this by simply running *five minutes at a time*.

Those who pace themselves—in marathons and in life—will be much more likely to succeed.

What about you?

- "One day at a time" is a favorite slogan of recovering addicts in 12-step programs. How might that be a useful motto in your own life as you learn to "pace the race"?

- How do you think the pace of your life would change if you were continually led by your personal values, and life purpose?

Knowing that
You're right beside
me in the new
horizon

Brace
for the
Final Kiss

*"Only in the agony of parting do we
look into the depths of love."*
– *George Eliot*

As I was writing a chapter for this book, I received a call from my mom one Monday evening. In fact, she called me twice, since I missed her first call.

Mom, who had suffered from Chronic Obstructive Pulmonary Disease (COPD) for years, didn't have much on her mind. She just wanted to tell me she loved me. And I assured her that I loved her too.

The following morning, I received an urgent phone call from my brother, John. Mother was in the hospital; the doctors said she could die within weeks—or hours.

I packed up a few clothes and in a little over eight hours I was in Mom's hospital room. Although she was lying unconscious and struggling to breathe, her face glowed and her skin appeared remarkably smooth and clear, like that of a little child. Oxygen and morphine eased her pain and helped her find some solace.

But Mom was dying.

I felt so helpless. For long minutes, I had no words.

Finally, I pressed closer to the bed, caressed Mom's face, gently arranged her hair, and grabbed her frail hand. Kissing her on the forehead, I said, "I love you, Mom." And somehow I felt her loving me back.

I had no idea this would be the final kiss...but it was. Mom passed into eternity mere moments after I kissed her goodnight.

In the hours that followed, Dad told us, "Mom had it harder than most, but she did the best she could. Now she can get some rest."

Some rest. Truly that was what Mom needed. Finding deep rest for our souls is the great antidote to life's challenges.

In the weeks after Mom's death, my mind was a whirlwind of thoughts...pleasant memories of her life...how much I missed her... the brevity of life...and my own mortality.

I remembered a song I wrote for a friend's funeral many years before:

In the laughter of a baby…the sky so clear and blue…
the gentle breezes blowing bring remembrance of you.
In the early hours at daybreak…with the passing of
each day…in the quiet of the evening I can hear the
angels say:

She's in the hands of God now, in the hands of God,
resting safely in His presence and His love.
With the changing of the seasons…realizing we're apart…
when I want to know the reasons for the void
within my heart.

I can hear the angels say:
She's in the hands of God now, in the hands of God, resting
safely in His presence and His love.

Yes, goodbyes are painful. But when I think of my relationship with Mom, I remember this line from the musical "Annie": "How lucky I am to have something that makes saying goodbye so hard."

What about you?

- Think about friends and loved ones who have died. Have you taken time to resolve their passing in your heart? If not, pause for a few minutes to do so now.

- We seldom know which kiss will be the "final" one for a loved one while on this earth. Make a list of friends and loved ones you need to express your love to.

Leaving my pain
in the past

Rewrite Your Personal History

"It's never too late—in fiction or in life—to revise."
– Nancy Thayer

As a kid in school, I believed everything written in my history textbooks. But my husband was a history major in college, and he opened my eyes to a sobering fact: Much of the history we read is one-sided, written from the perspective of the victors.

That's why Winston Churchill could quip, "History will be kind to me, for I intend to write it."

But it was a little disillusioning to realize I couldn't always take history books at face value.

Then I realized an even *more* alarming truth: People sometimes adopt a warped history of their own lives. And this negative view of their past holds them back from pursuing the positive dreams of their future.

I came to see that I had done this very thing myself, painting my past in much more negative colors than the facts would warrant. Sometimes I would negatively recount a past event with one of the participants, only to find that they had a much more positive recollection of what had happened.

I had allowed my personal history to become distorted. Although I wasn't sure the answer was to become a Pollyanna, pretending everything had always been wonderful, my negativity was certainly not helping me move on with a healthy perspective on my life.

When you read your old journals or diaries, do you see events that caused you to experience something akin to Post-Traumatic Stress Disorder (PTSD)? Were you hit by sudden lightning bolts when life was hard, people betrayed you, or you struggled to hold things together?

In many ways, this book has been a way to rewrite my personal history and make sense of the lessons along my journey. I wanted to grab the tools I've found and then share them with other women who, like me, sometimes wonder if we have what it takes to cope with a hurting and unraveling world.

I thought this would be an easy process, but it certainly hasn't been. For 10 years, I've written and rewritten my personal history, taking a look at life's lessons from every possible angle. Both good and bad memories kept flooding back, sometimes in confusing and bewildering ways. But I was committed to a relentless pursuit of that truth.

Gradually, I've been able to reframe the events of my past, seeing that even the negative things could have a redemptive purpose. The toxic thoughts and images of my mental camcorder have been replaced by constructive and healthy ones. To my amazement, I've come to see that even my worst experiences have often been blessings in disguise.

Novelist James A. Baldwin once observed, "People are trapped in history and history is trapped in them."

I set out in my life to prove him wrong. I'm not trapped in my history. I've been set free.

What about you?

- Take some time to review the "chapters" of your life so far. If you could choose one or two chapters to rewrite, which ones would they be?

- Compare stories with people who have been part of your life for a long time. Enjoy the different perspectives they bring to your shared experiences.

Feel the new
wind blowing

Epilogue:
Learn to Count
Your Blessings

*"Gratitude makes sense of our past, brings peace
for today, and creates a vision for tomorrow."*
– Melody Beatty

I'm learning to count my blessings—to focus on the good things I've learned along the way. I've discovered that there's no more powerful strategy to find emotional healing and peace.

I've come to realize that I need to think much less about what's wrong in my life and much more about the good things. As I learn to cultivate an attitude of gratitude, this is gradually dissolving my negativity and transforming my life from the inside out.

Countless authors have pointed out the amazing benefits of thankfulness. John Milton writes: "Gratitude bestows reverence, allowing us to encounter everyday epiphanies, those transcendent moments of awe that change forever how we experience life and the world." Wow. We can "encounter everyday epiphanies" through gratitude!

When I tell people that thankfulness has changed my life, they often want more specifics. How, exactly, do we develop a consistent, ongoing, "attitude of gratitude"? Good question! If we've developed a habit of grumbling and complaining for many years, this won't be an easy transition.

Here's what I suggest: Purchase a blank journal and make it your Gratitude Journal. No grumpiness, self-pity, or bellyaching are allowed in its pages—just thankfulness. And you need to write something at least once a week, if not daily.

If it seems too overwhelming to have an entire journal devoted to gratitude, it's also possible to simply write on your calendar or in your diary about the things you are thankful for. But the key is to be as consistent as possible, writing down your gratitude until it permanently transforms your attitude.

This discipline of thankfulness has been a huge factor in helping me cope with life.

Special Thanks

Right now, I want to count my blessings by thanking those who've helped shape me into the person I am today. At the risk of unintentionally omitting many dear friends and relatives who've been part of my life, I want to share my Gratitude List. As you can see from this long list, it took LOTS of people to make me who I am today!

• My "communities of support" along life's way... The 8th Street neighborhood in Cuyahoga Falls, St. Joseph's Catholic School, St. Francis DeSales High School, Capital University, Christian Community Church, The Health Made Simple Team, my many musical friends, The Live Well Carolina Leadership Team at Carolinas Health Care, Andy Calhoun, Eric Ellsworth and the Greater Charlotte YMCA, Kathrine Lee and The Source community.

• My counselors, coaches, and doctors (who helped me find wholeness in spirit, mind and body)... Dennis and Dr. Jen Clark, Doug Metzger, Dr. Beverly Rogers, Laura Barrett, Dr. Alvin Melvin, Dr. Neal Speight, Dr. Peter Tucker, Dr. Mike Meehan, Pastor Alex Clattenburg, Bob Samara, and Leighton Ford.

- My publishing team... In addition to my husband, I'm grateful for the support and feedback of friends who helped make this book happen: Lauri Kennemore, Hallie Hawkins, and Myra Brizendine Wilson who provided invaluable assistance with the first edition of the book; followed by Peg Robarchek, Fabi Preslar, and the amazingly creative team at SPARK Publications, including Brenda Cole, who designed the book cover.

- Special thanks to Autumn Lynn Photography for creating my headshot.

- Jim (my husband and friend)... Thanks for being a wonderful mentor, counselor and facilitator in my transformation. You've been a rock in my life and the glue in our family, and I am eternally grateful.

Finally, I'm grateful for each of YOU, the women in my community. I hope my journey has been an encouragement to you as you continue your own journey.

Let me leave you with this Irish Blessing:

May the road rise to meet you,
May the wind be always at your back.
May the sun shine bright upon your face,
The rain fall soft upon your fields;
And until we meet again,
May God hold you in the palm of His hand.

Free © Mary Buchan, 2006

It's so good to be free from the heaviness.
The weight's been lifted off, He's filled the emptiness
Of a weary heart longing to be free
From the pain and desperation that hovered over me.
And I now can move on to a better place.
The tears dried from my eyes, a smile now on my face.
And my tired soul is finally at rest,
As I look with expectation to days that lie ahead.
His Spirit blew upon me refreshing winds of peace.
The old has blown away and now the new has been released.
I will never be the same since His Spirit blew upon me.
I can see a window opening,
A second wind, the fragrance of new life,
Refreshing oxygen.
Past the veil of mystery, beyond the night,
I can see the new horizon with the dawning of the light.
A clean and holy breeze,
Flowing over me.

chorus
I'm free, I'm free,
His Spirit blew upon me
Refreshing winds of peace.
I'm free, I'm free,
The old has blown away,
The new has been released.
I'm free, I'm free,
Free!

To order additional copies of **Over iT** or learn about how **Mary Buchan** can help you make the rest of your life the best of your life, visit **MaryBuchan.com**.

Lifestyle RN
Make the Rest of your life the best of your life

About The Author

Mary Buchan is a Registered Nurse with a Bachelor's Degree in Science and Nursing from Capital University in Columbus, Ohio. After beginning her 25-year nursing career as a floor nurse on a medical-surgical unit, she became frustrated with traditional medicine's focus on disease treatment instead of disease prevention. She saw young people in their 20s, 30s, and 40s facing preventable conditions such as obesity, heart disease, and Type 2 diabetes.

Mary increasingly realized the importance of teaching people how to respect and care for their bodies in order to achieve vibrant health. This launched her on an exciting journey from traditional nursing to a new role as a Wellness Educator and Lifestyle Coach. She has helped hundreds of people lose weight, handle stress, increase their energy level, control their blood sugar, or boost their immune system.

As a wife, mother of three, nurse, blogger, and entrepreneur, Mary understands the needs of busy, professional women struggling with work-life balance. In addition to helping clients address their health issues, she often finds herself in the role of a Life Reinvention Coach—helping people rediscover their focus, purpose, and zest for living.

Mary has a special passion to help women age 40 and over navigate through the transitions of life, finding new meaning and fun as they fulfill their God-given design and mission. She loves coaching women through empty nests, menopause, career changes, and other types of reinvention. Regardless of the situation, she's convinced everyone can make the rest of their life the best of their life!

To sign up for a free newsletter or find out more about Mary's other resources and services, visit **MaryBuchan.com**.

Give Your Life a Makeover!

As you were reading *Over iT*, perhaps you thought of some "it" you still need to get over in your own life. Life Reinvention Workshops and coaching programs with Mary are your first steps towards taking control of your health, your stress level, your fitness, and your life's purpose!

Creative, customized coaching and workshops will help you target your personal goals...to feel great, look great, and get unstuck from anything hindering you from enjoying life to the fullest. (Limited opportunities available). With Mary's help, you can jump-start your health and fitness, take your life from tune-up to transformation, or experience the ultimate life makeover. Contact Mary today!

MaryBuchan.com
Feel great! Look great! Enjoy life!

Mary@MaryBuchan.com
855.792.7700

Lifestyle RN
Make the Rest of your life the best of your life